MICRO AND MACRO ECONOMICS

UNDERSTANDING THE BASICS OF ECONOMICS

–DR. SAMWEL NYAGUCHA ORESI –

DECEMBER 2014

New Generation Publishing

This book is dedicated to my dear wife, Moraa, and Lovely sons Onchoke, Ombuna, Mairura and Omwoyo

Acknowledgement

Special thanks go to my parents, Mr. and Mrs. Oresi, for their support since childhood. I would also like to express my sincere gratitude to my kindred Francisca, Mary, Ambrose, Ernest, Robert Jacqueline and the late James. I am also indebted to the Presbyterian University of East Africa, Kenya Institute of Management, Kisii University Campus, Mount Kenya University, Jomo Kenyatta University of Agriculture & Technology and The Railway Training Institute fraternities for having confidence in me and giving me the chance to exploit my talent. I also wish to thank my workmates, friends and relatives for their constant encouragement and support.

FOREWORD

Adam Smith is widely regarded as the father of modern economics. But he wasn't. The real founder may be someone most people have never heard of. More than 40 years before Adam Smith wrote "The Wealth of Nations," Richard Cantillon authored the "Essai sur la Nature du Commerce en General." Economics is the science that concerns itself with economies, from how societies produce goods and services to how they consume them. The assumptions that guide the study of economics, have changed dramatically throughout history. The publication of Adam Smith's the Wealth of Nations in 1776 is usually considered to mark the beginning of classical economics. The school was active into the mid-19th century and was followed by neoclassical economics in Britain beginning around 1870.

Economics is the study of how societies, governments, businesses, households, and individuals allocate their scarce resources. Our discipline has two important features. First, we develop conceptual models of behaviour to predict responses to changes in policy and market conditions. Second, we use rigorous statistical analysis to investigate these changes.

Economists are well known for advising the president and parliaments on economic issues, formulating policies at the

Central Banks, and analysing economic conditions for investment banks, brokerage houses, real estate companies, and other private sector businesses. They also contribute to the development of many other public policies including health care, welfare, and school reform and efforts to reduce inequality, pollution and crime.

The study of economics can also provide valuable knowledge for making decisions in everyday life. It offers a tool with which to approach questions about the desirability of a particular financial investment opportunity, whether or not to attend college or graduate school, the benefits and costs of alternative careers, and the likely impacts of public policies including universal health care and a higher minimum wage.

The art of work has been made simple to understand and it can be used by diploma, undergraduate and post-graduate students. The writer has also published books on human resource management, employee & industrial relations, economics, and research methods. Other question and answer books written are on Human Resource Management, Employee & Industrial Relations, Labour Economics, and Research Methods. If you have you have any critical review the author can be contacted through; P.O. Box 15785 00100 NRB, Mobiles: 0722857402/0735058551 or Email; samsamoresi@ymail.com

About the Author

The author, Dr. Samwel Nyagucha Oresi, is an Economist by profession with a bias in Labour Economics and a special interest in Human Resource Management. The liking of HRM is as a result of majoring in Labour Economics. He was born on 21st October 1966 and went to school while still very young. At the age of 4 he was in class 1 at Nyambera DOK (Kisii-Kenya). He later went to Kisii Primary School, from where he did his CPE in 1978. In 1979 he joined Kisii High School, from where he did his KCE in 1982. Having passed with good grades, he went to Kabarnet High School for A-levels and later proceeded to

India to pursue a B.A. degree course in Economics. He first joined St. Aloysius College, Jabalpur in 1983. He got his first degree, B.A. Economics, in 1986 from Poona University. He then completed his M.A. Economics in 1988 from Shivaji University. Being only 22 years of age at the time, and on the advice of his father, he decided to pursue his PhD, which he attained in 1994 from Shivaji University at the age of 28.

The author has worked with the Kenya Railways as the Corporate Planning Manager, Supplies & Procurement Manager and Human Resources Officer. He later on moved to lecturing and consultancy, which is his current occupation. The author has published books in Human Resources Management, Macro and Micro Economics, Labour Economics and Research Methods. He has also written question and answer books on economics, labour economics, employee relations &counselling, and research methods.

The art of work has been made simple to understand and it can be used by diploma, undergraduate and post-graduate students. The writer has also published books on human resource management, labour economics and research methods. Other question and answer books written are in Micro & Macro Economics, Labour Economics, Employee Relations & Counselling and Research Methods. If you have you have any critical review the author can be contacted through; P.O. Box 15785 00100 NRB, Mobiles: 0722857402/0736592713 or Email;

samsamoresi@ymail.com

CHAPTER ONE 1

CHAPTER TWO 28

CHAPTER THREE   69

CHAPTER FOUR   91

CHAPTER FIVE   141

CHAPTER SIX   **175**

CHAPTER SEVEN   198

CHAPTER EIGHT   205

CHAPTER NINE 223

CHAPTER TEN 265

CHAPTER ONE

INTRODUCTION

Economics

Economics does not have a generally accepted definition because it is considered an unfinished science. Over time, different economists have defined it differently. None of the definitions of economics captures the entire subject matter of modern economics, though they do throw some light on what economics is about. Some of those definitions are:

Adam Smith, in 1776, described economics as a study of the wealth of nations

Alfred Marshall defined economics as a study of mankind in the ordinary business life, especially how man obtains income and how he spends it

Robbins defined economics as a science of scarcity and choice – i.e. a study of human behaviour in relations between ends (wants) and means (resources)

Modern Definitions - Economics is a social science that deals with how man uses and distributes the scarce resources that have various uses to satisfy his wants. Economics as a social science studies the economic

1

behaviour of people and its consequences

Economics is a social science concerned with the production, distribution and consumption of goods and services.

Economics focuses on the behaviour and interactions of *economic* agents and how economies work.

Economics is the study of scarcity, the study of how people use resources and respond to incentives, or the study of decision-making. It often involves topics like wealth and finance, but it's not all about money. Economics is a broad discipline that helps us understand historical trends, interpret today's headlines, and make predictions about the coming years.

Types of Economics

There are two types of economics;

1. *Positive Economics*: This is concerned with the study of what is. It is based on facts which can be proved to be true or false: e.g. Kenya is a developing country – true: Sudan is highly developed false

2. *Normative Economics*: This is concerned with what ought to be. It is based on personal opinions, value judgments, cultural beliefs and not on facts, and cannot be proved to be true or false: e.g. the Kenya

Government should reduce its expenditure; it is bad for women to drink beer

Methods of Studying Economics

1. *Deductive Method*: This involves proceeding from the unknown to the known. A well-known and accepted generalization is taken and applied in a particular case. The economist begins with an hypothesis which may be a mere guess and then deduces (infers): e.g. all African countries are poor; Kenya is an African country; therefore Kenya is poor

2. *Inductive Method*: This involves proceeding from the known to the unknown. The method begins by observing, classifying facts and finally making a generalization: e.g. Kenya is a poor country; Tanzania is a poor country; Uganda is a poor country; Rwanda is a poor country, Burundi is a poor country; all these countries are in East Africa; therefore East Africa is a poor region

Branches of Economics

There are two branches of economics

1. Micro economics
2. Macro economics

Micro economics is the study of the actions and behaviour of the individual consumer, firm, worker, etc: e.g.

3

consuming a soda as an individual. It is concerned with the microscopic study of the various elements of the economic system and not with the system as a whole.

Macro economics is a relatively new branch of economics and it studies the working and performance of the economy as a whole. It deals with the actions and behaviour of the whole society/economy. It deals with aggregates: e.g. unemployment, national income, inflation etc. Macro economics is useful when seeking fiscal and monetary policies that help solve economic problems: e.g. unemployment, inflation, etc.

Objectives of Macro Economics

The objective of microeconomic theory is to analyse how individual decision-makers, both consumers and producers, behave in a variety of economic environments. The main objectives are;

1. To achieve full employment in the economy
2. To ensure that prices are stable in the economy
3. To achieve equilibrium in the balance of payments
4. To promote economic growth and development
5. To promote equal distribution of income in the economy

Specialised Branches of Economic Studies

1. *Economics of development*: This deals with the factors that determine the economic development and growth of a country, the causes of underdevelopment, unemployment and poverty

2. *Public economics*: This examines the economic role of the Government, sources of Government revenue, fiscal policy, etc.

3. *Monetary economics*: This studies the monetary affairs of the country, including demand for and supply of money

4. *International economics*: This deals with international trade and international monetary institutions

5. *Industrial economics*: This is concerned with the working, structures and growth of the industrial sector

6. *Labour economics*: This branch deals with labour issues as a factor of production

7. *Economic history*: This studies the past economic records of a country or group of countries: e.g. the industrial revolution, the great depression, etc

8. *Econometrics*: This is the study of statistical and mathematical techniques applied to economic data

9. *History of economic thought*: This is the study of the evolution and development of economic thoughts and ideas

10. *Comparative economic systems*: This is a comparative study of economic systems; capitalist, socialist and mixed economies

11. *Regional economics*: This studies the development of various regions of a country; balanced and imbalanced growth

12. *Industrial finance*: This is concerned with the development and working of the financial sector

13. *Environmental economics*: This examines how industrial growth affects the natural environment of the country and the globe e.g. global warming, pollution, etc.

14. *Managerial economics*: This studies how economic theories, concepts and tools of analysis can be applied to business decision making and to understanding the business environment of a country

Basic Economic Concepts (Main Issues Discussed In Economics)

The main issues discussed in economics are: Wants, Scarcity, Choice, Scale of Preference and Opportunity Cost.

Wants

These are human desires or needs. Human needs are unlimited and insatiable: e.g. the desire for food, housing, cars, etc. They keep on recurring and that is why they cannot be satisfied. Human wants are divided into two categories: *Basic human wants* – These are things that man can't do without (necessities) such as food, clothing, shelter, education, etc.; *Secondary human wants* – these are human wants that man can do without. They are called luxuries. They make life more comfortable: e.g. cars, radios, beer, etc.

Scarcity

This applies to a situation where the supply of an item is less than the amount required. In real life, human wants are unlimited but the resources to meet them are limited and this creates scarcity

Choice

Because human wants are many and the resources to meet them limited, a person or country has to make a choice of which ones to satisfy first. The most important need is prioritised. Such a selection is called choice

Scale of Preference

The actual making of choices requires the ranking of goods and services. Such ranking helps to identify more and less urgent wants. A list of wants in order of priority is called a scale of preference

Opportunity Cost

This is the value of the best alternative not chosen: e.g. a person may decide to buy a car instead of buying a house. The value of the house is the opportunity cost. It is also known as opportunity lost. Opportunity cost is important in the following ways;

1. Consumers decide what to consume
2. Producers decide what to produce
3. Government decides where to invest
4. Government decides what to produce
5. International trade then decides what to specialise in
6. Money and banking

Basic Economic Problems

The economic problem – sometimes called the basic or central economic problem – asserts that an economy's finite resources are insufficient to satisfy all human wants and needs. It assumes that human wants are unlimited, but the means to satisfy human wants are limited. Economic problems arise because of scarcity and choice, since human wants are unlimited and the resources to produce them limited. A choice must be made as to which wants are to be produced first using scarce resources which have alternative uses. Due to scarcity and choice, economists ask the following questions;

1. What to Produce and in What Quantities?

This question addresses the issue of which goods to produce and in what quantities, given the scarce resources which have alternative uses

The first central problem of an economy is to decide what goods and services are to be produced and in what quantities. This involves allocation of scarce resources in relation to the composition of total output in the economy. Since resources are scarce, the society has to decide about the goods to be produced: wheat, cloth, roads, television, power, buildings, and so on.

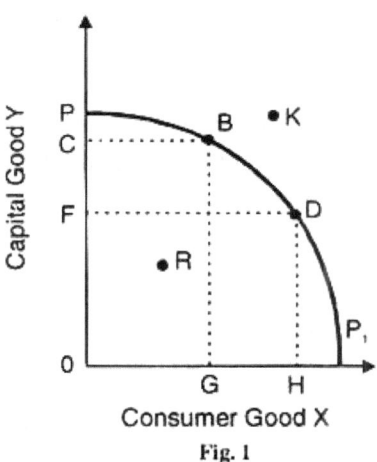

Fig. 1

Once the nature of goods to be produced is decided, then their quantities are to be decided. How many tonnes of wheat, how many televisions, how many million kws of power, how many buildings, etc. Since the resources of the economy are scarce, the problem of the nature of goods and their quantities has to be decided on the basis of priorities or preferences of the society. If the society gives priority to the production of more consumer goods now, it will have less in the future. A higher priority on capital goods implies less consumer goods now and more in the future. But since resources are scarce, if some goods are produced in larger quantities, some other goods will have to be produced in smaller quantities.

This problem can also be explained with the help of the production possibility curve as shown in the figure above

Suppose the economy produces capital goods and consumer goods. In deciding the total output of the economy, the society has to choose that combination of capital goods and consumer goods which is in keeping with its resources.

It cannot choose the combination R which is inside the production possibility curve PP_1 because it reflects economic inefficiency of the system in the form of unemployment of resources. Nor can it choose the combination R which is outside the current production possibilities of the society. The society lacks the resources to produce this combination of capital goods and consumer goods.

It will, therefore, have to choose among the combinations B, E, or D which give the highest level of satisfaction. If the society decides to have more capital goods, it will choose combination B; and if it wants more consumer goods, it will choose combination D.

How to Produce these Goods?

This refers to the method to be used in production of goods. The cost and availability of inputs determine the method of production. There are two main methods of production;

   a. Labour intensive, which involves the use of more units of labour than capital in the production process

   b. Capital intensive, which involves the use of more capital units than labour in the production process

The next basic problem of an economy is to decide about the techniques or methods to be used in order to produce the required goods. This problem is primarily dependent upon the availability of resources within the economy.

If land is available in abundance, it may have extensive cultivation. If land is scarce, intensive methods of cultivation may be used. If labour is in abundance, it may use labour-intensive techniques; while in the case of labour shortage, capital-intensive techniques may be used.

The technique to be used also depends upon the type and

quantity of goods to be produced. For producing capital goods and large outputs, complicated and expensive machines and techniques are required. On the other hand, simple consumer goods and small outputs require small and less expensive machines and comparatively simple techniques.

Further, it has to be decided what goods and services are to be produced in the public sector and what goods and services in the private sector. But in choosing between different methods of production, those methods should be adopted which bring about an efficient allocation of resources and increase the overall productivity in the economy.

Suppose the economy is producing certain quantities of consumer and capital goods at point A on PP curve in Figure 2. y adopting new techniques of production, given the supplies of factors, the productive efficiency of the economy increases. As a result, the PP_0 curve shifts outwards to P_1P_1.

It leads to the production of more quantities of consumer and capital gods from point A on PP_0 curve to point C of PP with be the new production possibility curve and the economy will move from point A to B where more of both the goods are produced.

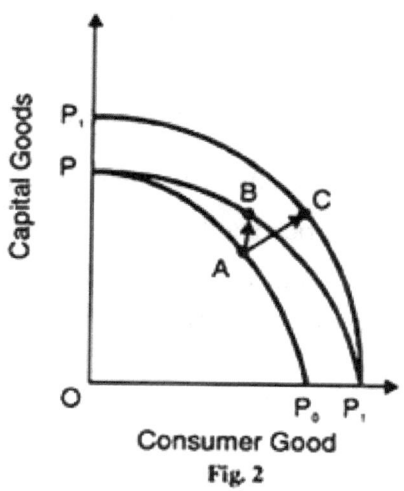

Consumer Good

Fig. 2

For whom is the Goods Produced?

This question addresses the distribution of national income among different groups of people in the economy: i.e. who should get what and how much. The principle of equity must be considered: e.g. the Government can spend money on education to benefit society

The third basic problem to be decided is the allocation of goods among the members of the society. The allocation of basic consumer goods or necessities and luxuries comforts and among the household takes place on the basis of among the distribution of national income.

Whosoever possesses the means to buy the goods may have then. A rich person may have a large share of the luxuries goods, and a poor person may have more quantities of the basic consumer goods he needs. This problem is illustrated in Figure 3 where the production possibility curve PP shows the combinations of luxuries and necessaries.

At point B on the PP curve, the economy is producing more of luxuries OC for the rich and less of necessaries OC for the at whereas at point D more of necessaries OH are being produced for the poor and less of luxuries OF for the rich.

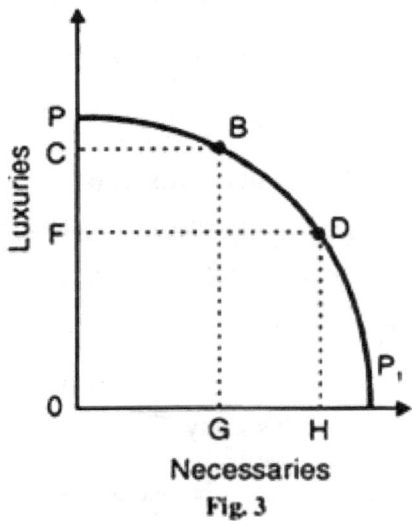

Fig. 3

2. How Efficiently are the Resources being Utilised?

This is one of the important basic problems of an economy because having made the three earlier decisions, the society has to see whether the resources it owns are being utilised fully or not. In case the resources of the economy are lying idle, it has to find out ways and means to utilise them fully.

14

If the idleness of resources, say manpower, land or capital, is due to their male allocation, the society will have to adopt such monetary, fiscal, or physical measures whereby this is corrected. This is illustrated in Figure 4 where the production possibility curve PP reflects idle resources within the economy at point A, while the production possibility curve P_1P_1 reflects the full utilisation of the resources at point B or C.

It is for the society to decide whether to produce more capital goods at point B or more consumer goods at point C, or both at point D at the level of full employment represented by the In an economy where the available resources are being fully utilised, it is characterised by technical efficiency or full employment.

To maintain it at this level, the economy must always be increasing the output of some goods and services by giving up something of others.

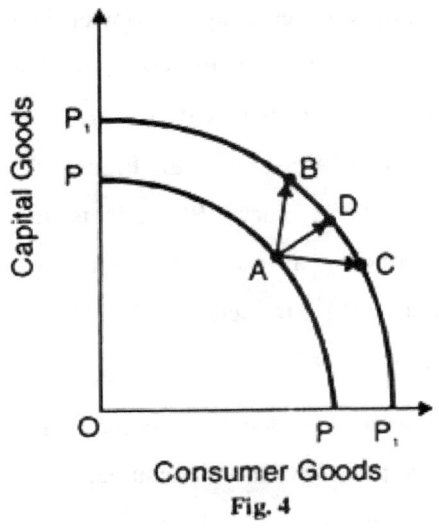

Fig. 4

3. Is the Economy Growing?

A provision must be made for the economy to grow. Neither individuals nor society should use all the scarce resources on current consumption. A provision must be made in terms of allocating resources for investment to produce goods and services in future The last and the most important problem is to find out whether the economy is growing through time or is it stagnant. If the economy is stagnant at any point inside the production possibility curve, says in Figure 5, it has to be moved on to the production possibility curve PP whereby the economy now produces larger quantities of consumer goods and capital goods.

Economic growth takes place through a higher rate of capital formation which consists of replacing existing capital goods with new and more productive ones by adopting more efficient production techniques or through innovations.

This leads to the outward shifting of the production possibility curve from PP to P_1P_1; (in Figure 5). The economy moves, say after 5 years, from point A to B or C or D on the P_1P_1 curve. Point C represents the situation where larger quantities of both consumer and capital goods are produced in the economy. Economic growth enables the economy to have more of both the goods.

Fig. 5

All these central problems of an economy are interrelated and interdependent. They arise from the fundamental economic problems of scarcity of means and multiplicity of ends which lead to the problem of choice or economizing of resources.

Scope of Economics (Main Activities Discussed In Economics)

This refers to the subject matter discussed in economics. The main activities discussed in economics include;

1. *Production* – This is the process of creating goods and services to satisfy human wants. It is the creation of utility/satisfaction

2. *Consumption* – This is the utilization of goods and services which have been produced to satisfy human wants

3. *Distribution* – This is the process of paying out rewards to the factors/resources used in production

4. *Exchange* – This is the transfer of ownership of production from one person to another

Economic Systems and Resource Allocation

An *Economic system* is a set of institutional arrangements whose role is to employ the scarce resources in the most efficient way to satisfy the needs of society

Resource allocation means the apportionment of the scarce resources available among the many alternative uses so as to achieve maximum satisfaction. At national level, resources can be allocated by either private individuals, Government or by both. Depending on who owns and allocates resources (i.e. whether private individuals or the Government) we have three types of economic systems

1. Free Market/Capitalist Economy
2. Planned/Command Economy
3. Mixed Economy

Free Market Economy

In this type of economy all resources are owned and are allocated by private individuals. It has the following features:

1. All the resources are owned by private individuals
2. Private individuals decide what, how, how much and for whom to produce
3. There is free enterprise, meaning there is no price control, no taxes etc.
4. The aim of private individuals is to make profit
5. The allocation of resources is guided by price mechanism, i.e. the market forces of demand and supply
6. The economy is divided into two parts; the haves and the have-nots
7. There are many buyers and sellers
8. There is uneven distribution of wealth in the economy

9. There is competition among producers: e.g. they cut prices to sell more goods

Advantages of a Free Market Economy

1. People are encouraged to work hard because there are opportunities to accumulate wealth
2. Competition among producers leads to the production of high-quality products
3. Competition leads to proper resource allocation, since there is no political interference
4. There is freedom of choice in terms of how to spend their money, the type of business to set up, for whom to work etc.
5. The price mechanism ensures that there is no over-production or shortages of goods and services
6. There are many sellers, hence consumers enjoy a variety of products
7. Sometimes market forces ensure that consumers get goods at lower prices when there is excess supply

Disadvantages of a Free Market Economy

1. There is an unequal distribution of wealth/income in the economy whereby the rich have a lot and the poor little or nothing
2. There is no room to provide public goods for the benefit of society as a whole
3. It may lead to the development of monopolies, which

will in turn exploit customers through overcharging

4. It may lead to inflation, since prices are not controlled

5. Unfair competition may lead to the collapse of weak firms, which may cause unemployment

6. It may lead to inefficiency and wastage in production

7. Due to the profit motive, negative externalities such as pollution may be experienced

8. It may entail illegal and harmful production, since there is no Government control

9. Economic instability

Command/Planned Economy

This is a Government-controlled economy and it has the following features:

1. The resources are owned by the Government

2. There is no free enterprise: i.e. there is price control, payment of taxes etc.

3. There are no private monopolies

4. Resources are allocated by the Government or an agent of the State

5. There is equal distribution of wealth in the economy

6. Prices are determined by the Government

7. The main objective of the Government is not to make profits but to maximise social welfare

8. Economic stability

9. Illegal and harmful goods cannot be produced

Advantages

1. There is equal distribution of wealth and income in the economy

2. There are no private monopolies to exploit customers by overcharging them

3. The Government provides public goods which benefit society as a whole

4. The aim of producers is not to make profits, so they take care not to have negative externalities

5. Firms operate on a large scale and thus enjoy economies of scale

6. The Government provides more basic needs and fewer luxuries

Disadvantages

1. Consumers have no choice because they have no control over what is to be produced

2. Goods and services produced are of low quality because there is no competition

3. Consumers lack freedom of choice in what to consume, how to spend their money etc.

4. Price controls may lead to over-consumption, which create shortages and thus rationing

5. It is difficult for the Government to know the needs of the entire economy

Mixed Economy

This is where some resources are owned and allocated by the Government and some by private individuals. Private individuals aim at maximizing profits while the Government aims at maximizing the social welfare of the people. (Advantages and Disadvantages can be deduced from free market economy and command economy).

Consumer Sovereignty

In a free-market economy the consumer is treated like a King (Queen). Producers produce goods according to the needs of the consumers. The consumer determines what is to be produced in the economy. It is the situation in an economy where the desires and needs of consumers control the output of producers. The theory suggests that consumers, not producers, are the best judge of what products benefit them the most. Due to the fact that consumer markets depend so heavily on demand, producers must monitor the needs of these individuals if they want their products to have any chance at success.

Limitations of Consumer Sovereignty

1. *The Size of Income* – The size of income determines who gets what and who doesn't. Those with high income get the goods they want and those with low income cannot get the goods they want

2. *Advertising and Pressure from Salesmen* – These sometimes determine what the consumer buys. One may end up buying what one has not planned for

3. *Government Control* – Sometimes the Government controls or determines what is to be consumed, e.g. harmful products

4. *Standardised Products* – This kind of product treats all consumers equally and hence individual needs are not considered, e.g. music in public transport

5. *Social Factors* – Some consumers consume or do not consume goods because of their religious and cultural beliefs; e.g. Muslims and consumption of pork or Hindus and consumption of beef

6. *Climatic or Environmental Factors* – At times, due to adverse weather, people are forced to consume goods to cope with the adverse conditions: e.g. in Russia one may be forced to take vodka against one's wish in order to keep warm

7. *Ignorance* – Due to ignorance, a consumer may end up consuming a commodity s/he did not want to. One may be duped or conned into buying a commodity that is not of one's choice

8. *Type of economic system* – In a planned or command economy the Government determines what is to be consumed, since it is the only producer

9. ***Existence of monopoly*** – Similar to the command economy, where there is a monopolist, the buyers have no variety or choice.

10. **Tax Structure**- The prevailing tax structure in the economy may adversely affect the consumption of the consumer and his choice may get restricted. This point is only a corollary from the two points already stated, viz., size of money-income and restriction by government.

Consumer's Sovereignty is a myth

It is clear that there are many limitations on the sovereignty of the consumer. He is not all powerful even in a capitalistic economy. Apparently he may seem to enjoy sovereign powers in normal times, but very frequently his sovereignty reduces into nothing. Socialists who attack capitalism tooth and nail, decry that consumer's sovereignty is a myth. They contend that the consumer is exploited by monopolistic capitalists and instead of being sovereign, he is reduced to the position of a slave, a milch-cow in the hands of producers.

Consumer's Sovereignty is not desirable

Socialists further argue that even taking it for granted that there is consumer's sovereignty, it is not desirable to have such a sovereignty. It is not conducive to the larger interest of the society.

Consumers, according to socialists, are irrational, emotional and quite unfit and unqualified to make correct choices. If they are allowed to exercise, their free will, it may lead to wrong and uneconomic utilization of resources. Socialists oppose full freedom to consumers on the assumption that the consumers are not only irrational, but they do not know their own interests.

Allowing full freedom in choices, the consumers are likely to injure themselves in the process and it is the State which should direct consumption and production, as it knows the interest of the consumer better. This is a very extreme and pessimistic view of socialists, reflecting the poor opinion of them about the consumers. May be the consumer is a poor judge when faced with a bewildering variety of goods which are close substitutes and perhaps he may make an irrational choice; but in normal circumstances, the consumer will exercise his choice correctly, as he is rational. This is more so if it is a question of choosing the necessaries of life.

The consumer will exercise his choice correctly in food, clothing and other normal amenities of life. He may become irrational in cases of drugs, alcoholic liquor and commodities which are called luxuries and semi-luxuries and choose in the wrong way. In these areas, the State can direct the consumer to be rational in choosing for consumption.

Conclusion

To conclude the consumer's power is not absolute. He is neither a sovereign nor a slave. There are some limitations in exercising the choice by the consumer. He is a source of profit and his wishes cannot be altogether ignored. It pays a producer to humor and flatter a consumer. He may not be a sovereign; but he is like a heroine to be wooed. Progress depends on alert and responsive consumer and prudent producer.

CHAPTER TWO

DEMAND ANALYSIS

The Theory of Demand

Demand is the quantity of goods and services that consumers are willing and able to purchase at a given market price (that is, desire backed by willingness and ability to pay). In economics we talk of effective demand. For effective demand to take place, the consumer should be willing and able to purchase a good or service at a given market price. Willingness alone is merely desire, because one may not be able to pay. People demand goods and services because they have utility. *Utility* is the satisfaction derived from the consumption of a good or service; the ability of a good or service to satisfy human wants; or the usefulness of a good or service

Categories of Utility

Total Utility – is the total satisfaction derived from the consumption of a good or service

Ante utility – is the expected satisfaction from the consumption of a good or service

Post Utility – is the actual satisfaction derived after consumption of a good or service

Marginal Utility – is the additional satisfaction derived from consuming an extra unit of a good or service

Negative Utility – is the dissatisfaction derived from the excess consumption of a good or service

The Law of Diminishing Marginal Utility

The law of diminishing marginal utility is central to cardinal utility analysis of consumer behaviour. The law of diminishing marginal utility states that marginal utility decreases as consumption increases, provided the consumption of all other goods remains constant. Utility is measured in utile. As one consumes a commodity, one will gradually want less of that commodity. If one is very thirsty and drinks water, the second glass will not be as satisfying as the first. Negative utility can occur if there is excess consumption. This can be explained by the use of a table and graph as follows:

Glasses of Water	Total Utility (TU)	Marginal Utility (MU)
0	0	0
1	40	40
2	60	20
3	70	10
4	75	5
5	75	0
6	65	-10

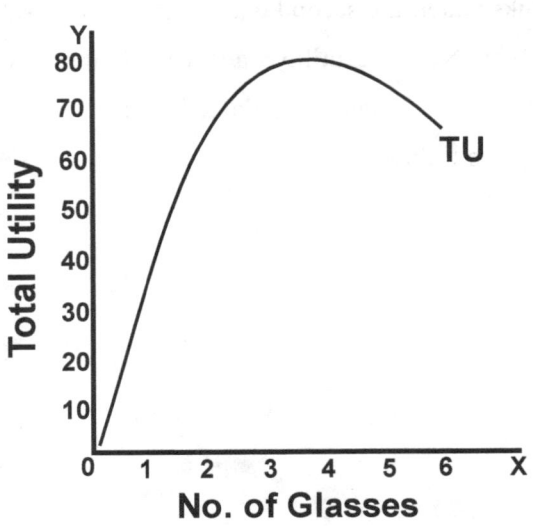

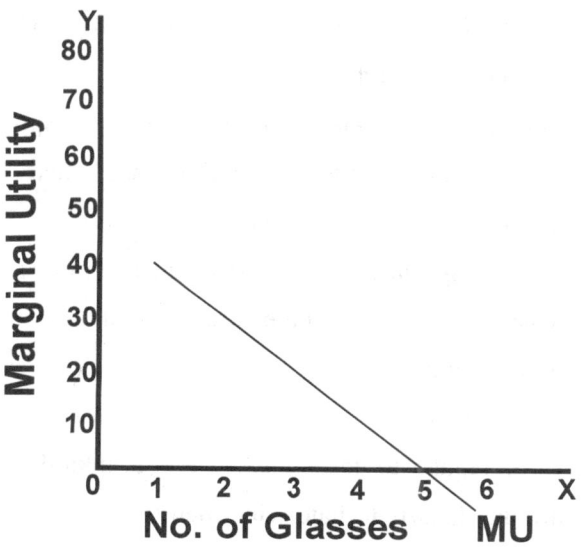

Assumptions of the Law

1. **Rationality** – It is assumed that the consumer is rational. The aim is to maximize utility subject to availability of income

2. **Constant marginal utility for money** – It is assumed that the marginal utility of money used for purchasing goods remains constant. If the marginal utility of money changes with the increase or decrease in income, it cannot yield measurement of the marginal utility of the good

3. **Diminishing marginal utility** – The utility gained from successive units of a commodity diminishes in a given time period

4. ***Utility is additive*** – The total utility of each commodity is additive

5. ***Consumption is continuous*** – The consumption of the commodity must be continuous. If there is an interval the law does not hold

6. ***Suitable quantity*** – The units consumed must be of reasonable quantity. If they are too small then the law will not apply

7. ***Character of the consumer does not change*** – This is in regard to tastes, e.g. of a drunkard. If the drunkard starts to hate wine then the law will apply but if he develops a liking then it will not hold

8. ***No changes to fashion*** – If customs and tastes change then the law will not apply

9. ***No change in the price of the commodity*** – The price of the commodity should not change as more units are consumed. If the price decreases then the law will not hold

Exemptions to the Law

1. ***Beer*** – The subsequent beers have a higher utility. However, even this commodity has a limit and may cause negative utility

2. ***Money*** – The more you have the more you need

3. ***Greed for fame***

4. ***Jewellery collection by women***

5. ***The size of units consumed*** – If one is taking water using a spoon then the second spoon may be more satisfying than the first one

6. **Rationality** - Requires that the behavior and mental condition of the consumer should be normal during consumption period.

7. **Continuity in consumption** - Implies that the consumption of a good should be continuous. In other words, this assumption states that the time interval between the consumption of units must be short.

8. **Consistency in consumer's tastes** - Implies that the tastes and preferences of consumers must remain same during the consumption period. If the tastes of consumers change, the law may not hold.

Importance of the Law

1. Basis of economic laws:

   Various laws of economics are derived on the basis of marginal utility. For example law of demand, law of substitution, concept of consumers' surplus, etc.

2. Importance to the finance minister:

   This law helps finance minister to formulate fiscal policy. Finance minister impose high tax to the rich people and low tax to the poor people on the basis of the law.

3. Importance to consumer:

This law is useful to consumer because by consuming the more units of commodity, satisfaction starts to decline. On the basis of this law consumer spends his/her money to purchase suitable quantity of commodity which maximizes his/her satisfaction.

4. Useful to reduce unequal distribution of wealth: This law is useful for the government to reduce the unequal distribution of wealth because marginal utility of wealth for poor is high and for rich is low. So to maintain M.U of wealth government imposes the progressive tax (i.e. high tax to rich and low tax to poor).

5. Price determination: This law is useful to determine the price. Basically price of commodity depends on utility so if seller wants to sell more quantity he must reduce the price or for more quantity to sell a unit price is low.

The Law of Demand

This sates that holding other things constant (ceteris paribus) as the price of goods increases, demand decreases and vice versa. There is an inverse or negative relationship between price and demand. The law of demand can be explained by the use of a Demand Schedule or Demand Curve

Demand Schedule

This is a table showing quantities of goods demanded at different market prices:

Price Per Kilo (Kshs)	Quantity Demanded (Kg)
100	20
150	15
200	10
250	5

Demand Curve

This is a curve showing quantities of goods demanded at different market prices:

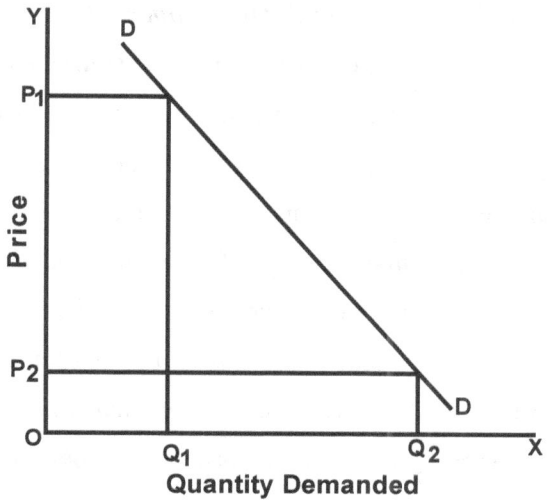

The demand curve is downward, sloping from left to right, showing a negative relationship between the quantity demanded and the price. As the price increases demand decreases and vice versa.

Factors Affecting Demand

1. *The Price of the Good in Question* – As the price of the good increases, it means that the purchasing power of the consumer deceases; thus demand decreases and vice versa

2. *Size of Income of Consumers* – As the size of income of consumers increases, the purchasing power increases; thus, demand increases

3. *Changes in Population* – As the population increases, demand increases and vice versa

4. *The Price of Other Related Goods* – Goods can be Substitutes or Complementary. *Substitute goods* are those goods which serve the same purpose and one good can be replaced easily with another; e.g. butter and margarine, tea and coffee. If the price of tea increases while that of coffee remains the same the demand for coffee increases and that for tea decreases, because it will become cheaper to most consumers, and vice versa. *Complementary goods* are those goods which must always be consumed together, e.g. car and petrol. If the demand for cars

increases, the demand for petrol also increases

5. ***Distribution of Income*** – If income is equally distributed it means many people will be able to buy goods, and demand increases, and vice versa

6. ***Governments Policy*** – Taxes imposed on products make them expensive and demand decreases. Subsidies given by the Government make the goods cheaper and demand increases

7. ***Future Expectation*** – If the consumers expect a shortage or a rise in prices in future, demand increases now and decreases in future, and vice versa

8. ***Seasons*** – Some goods are in high demand during some seasons, e.g. success cards during exams, calendars in December, etc.

9. ***Weather and Climatic Conditions*** – Some goods are in high demand during some weather conditions; e.g. umbrellas during rainy weather, fans and fridges during hot weather

10. ***Tastes and Preferences*** – When tastes and preferences change in favour of some commodity, demand increases and vice versa. A good example is the demand for Nokia phones.

Tastes and preferences are further determined by:

a) ***Gender*** – Some goods are purely meant for women and others purely for men

b) *Age* – Some goods are meant for babies, others for youth and others for old people

c) *Fashion* – Goods in fashion always have high demand compared to outdated ones

d) *Religion* – Some goods are demanded or not demanded because of religious beliefs

A Movement along the Demand Curve

This is caused by a change in price of a good which in turn leads to a change in the quantity demanded of that good. A movement along the demand curve means a movement of points of quantity demanded of a good along the same demand curve. This is also known as change in quantity demanded.

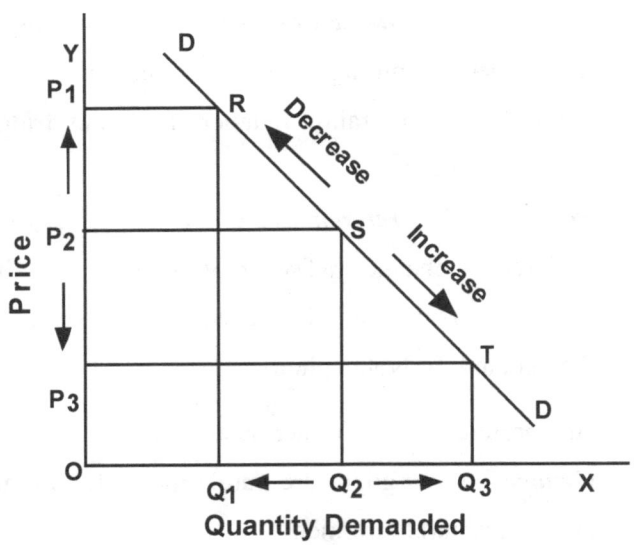

When the price increases from Pe to P1, the quantity demanded decreases from Qe to Q1, and this leads to a movement from point S to R along the same demand curve. When the price decreases from Pe to P2, the quantity demanded increases from Qe to Q2, and this leads to a movement from point S to T along the same demand curve.

A Shift in the Demand Curve

This is caused by changes in determinants of demand other than the price of that good, e.g. changes in income, population, etc. When other determinants of demand, apart from price, change, a change in demand causes the whole demand curve to shift. This is also known as change in demand.

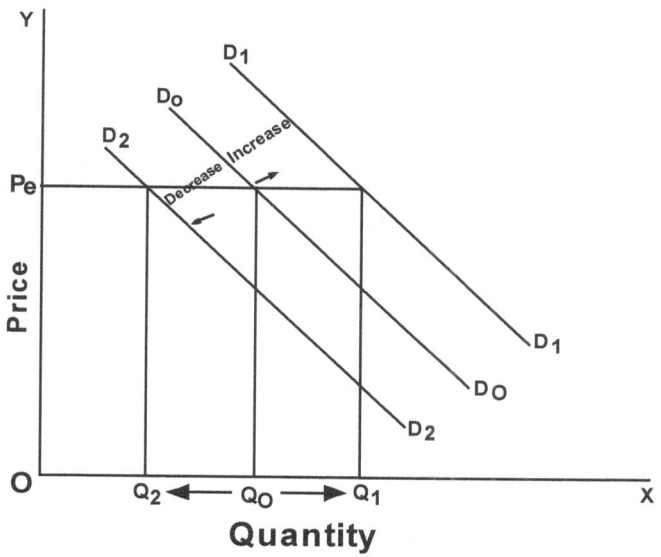

Assume that the original demand curve is D0. When determinants of demand change in favour of a commodity (e.g. rise in population), demand increases. An increase in demand causes the whole demand curve to shift upwards to the right from D0 to D1 as demand increases from Q0 to Q1. A decrease in demand causes the whole demand curve to shift downwards to the left from D0 to D2 as demand decreases from Q0 to Q2.

Abnormal Demand Curves

In certain case the law of demand does not apply. With an increase in income the demand curve slopes downwards and with an increase in price it slopes upwards. Such cases include:

Inferior goods

These are goods such that, when income increases, their demand decreases and vice versa. The demand curve slopes downwards, showing a negative relationship between quantity demanded and income. This can happen for goods such as second-hand clothes, public transport, sukuma wiki, etc.

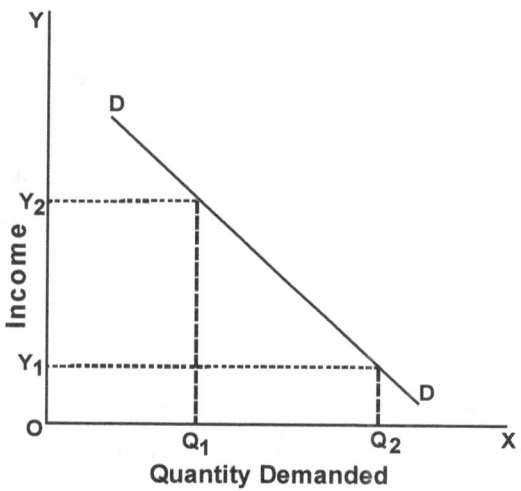

Luxury/Prestige goods

These are the goods such that, when price increases, demand also increases. They have an upward-sloping demand curve, e.g. expensive clothes, cars, radios etc.

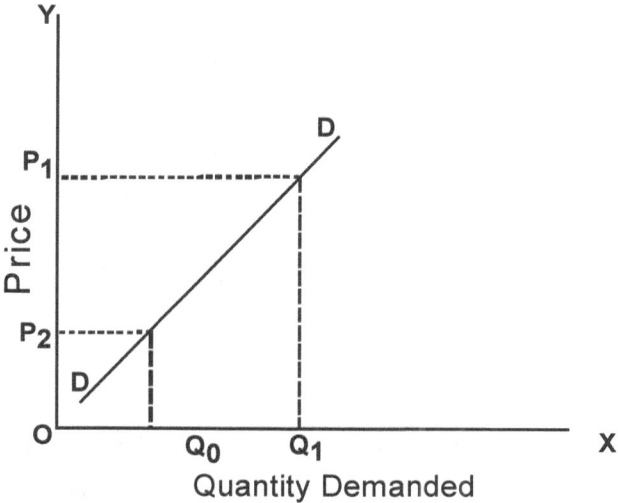

The reasons for this behaviour are that:

1. Some people link the price and quality such that the higher the price the higher the quality

2. Some people buy expensive things to maintain their status in society or to be seen as queens and kings and to be feared by others

Giffen goods

These are the basic necessities among poor people, e.g. maize in Africa and rice in Asia. Giffen goods have a backward bending demand curve.

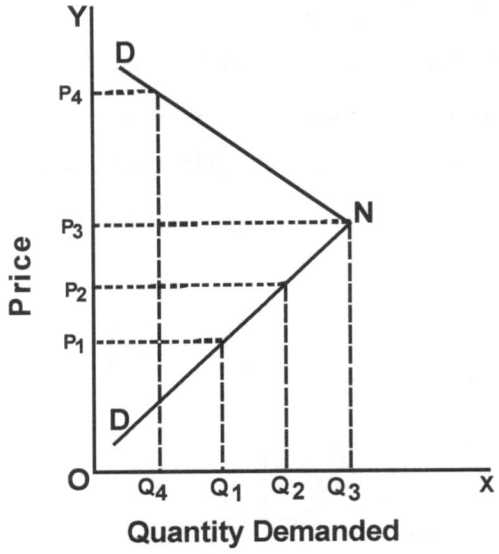

Initially, when the price increases from P1 to P2, demand increases from Q1 to Q2. This is because the poor start to eliminate luxuries, e.g. cooking oil, butter, and use the

money to buy more of a Giffen good, e.g. maize. Further increase, e.g. at P3, demand starts decreasing. At P4, quantity demanded is Q4. This is because the poor person can eliminate no more luxuries and has no more money to buy Giffen goods. As a result, the Giffen goods have a backward-bending demand curve.

ELASTICITY OF DEMAND

This refers to the responsiveness of demand to a change in one of the determinants of demand, e.g. price, income, etc. It measures the extent by which the quantity demanded of goods changes due to a change in one of the determinants of demand.

There are three types of elasticity of demand:

1. Price elasticity of demand
2. Income elasticity of demand
3. Cross elasticity of demand

Price Elasticity of Demand

This refers to the responsiveness of demand due to a change in the price of a good. It measures the extent by which the quantity demanded of a good changes, due to a change in price of that good. There are four methods of calculating price elasticity of demand

Method 1: Percentage Method

$$P.E.D = \frac{\% \text{ change in Qd}}{\% \text{ change in P}}$$

$$= \frac{\text{New Qd} - \text{old Qd} \times 100}{\text{Old Qd}} \div \frac{\text{New P-old P} \times 100}{\text{Old P}}$$

Example

Following a price increase of bananas from Kshs. 5 to Kshs. 8, the quantity demanded for bananas decreased from 35 to 30 per week. Calculate the price elasticity of demand

$$P.E.D = \frac{\% \Delta \text{ in Qd}}{\% \Delta \text{ in Qd}}$$

$$= \frac{\text{New Qd} - \text{Old Qd.}}{\text{Old Qo}} \div \frac{\text{New P-OldP} \times 100}{\text{Old P}}$$

$$= \frac{30\text{-}35 \times 100}{35} \div \frac{8\text{-}5 \times 100}{5}$$

$$= \frac{5}{35} \times 100 \div \frac{3}{5} \times 100$$

$$= \frac{500}{35} \times \frac{5}{3} \quad = 0.2$$

Method 2: Proportionate

$$P.E.D = \frac{\text{proportionate } \Delta \text{ Qd}}{\text{Proportionate } \Delta \text{ in price}}$$

$$= \frac{\text{New Qd} - \text{old Qd}}{\text{Old Qd}} \div \frac{\text{New p-old p}}{\text{Old p}}$$

$$= \frac{30 - 35}{35} \div \frac{8 - 5}{5}$$

$$= {}^{-5}/_{35} \div {}^{3}/_{5}$$

$$= {}^{-5}/_{35} \div {}^{5}/_{3}$$

$$= {}^{-5}/_{21}$$

$$= -0.2$$

Interpretation

The value -0.2 means that when the price increases by 1%, quantity demanded decreases by 0.2%. The price elasticity of demand is always negative because there is a negative relationship between quantity demanded and price. As the price increases, demand decreases and vice versa.

N.B. If the answer is positive then the good consumed is not a normal good but a luxury item.

Method 3: Point Elasticity of Demand

This is the proportionate change in demand due to a change in price at a particular point on the same demand curve

Formula:

$$\text{P.E.D} = \frac{\Delta Qd}{\text{Original Qd}} \div \frac{\Delta p}{\text{Original P}}$$

$$\frac{\text{New Qd} - \text{Old Qd}}{\text{Old Qd}} \div \frac{\text{New P} - \text{Old P}}{\text{Old P}}$$

Example

As a result of price decrease of a good from Kshs. 10 to Kshs. 5 the quantity demanded increased from 100 to 200 units. Calculate the point elasticity of demand.

$$\text{P.E.D} = \frac{\Delta Qd}{Qd_o} \div \frac{\Delta P}{P_o}$$

$$= \frac{Qd_1 - Qdo}{Qdo} \div \frac{P_1 - P_o}{P_o}$$

$$= \frac{200 - 100}{100} \div \frac{5 - 10}{10}$$

$$= {}^{100}/_{100} \div - {}^{5}/_{10}$$

$$= {}^{100}/_{100} \div {}^{10}/_{-5}$$

$$= 1 \times -2$$

$$= -2$$

Method 4: Arc Elasticity

This is the elasticity of demand between two points along the same demand curve

Formula:

$$\frac{\Delta Qd}{\dfrac{Q_1 + Q_2}{2}} \div \frac{\Delta P}{\dfrac{P_1 + P_2}{2}}$$

$$\frac{\Delta Qd}{\dfrac{Q_1 + Q_2}{2}} \quad x \quad \frac{\dfrac{P_1 + P_2}{2}}{\Delta p}$$

$$= \frac{Qd_2 - Qd_1}{Q1 + Q2} \quad x \quad \frac{P1 + P2}{P2 - P1}$$

Example:

Original Q 1=100P1=10

Q2=200P2 = 5

$$= \frac{200 - 100}{100 + 200} \quad X \quad \frac{10 + 5}{5 - 10}$$

$$\frac{100}{300} \quad X \quad \frac{15}{-5}$$

$= {}_{5/-5}$

$= -1$

1. Degrees/Categories of Elasticity of Demand

Depending on the value obtained, we have various categories of elasticity of demand.

Perfectly Inelastic Demand

This occurs when a change in price doesn't cause any change in demand. The value = 0 Demand is the same at all prices, e.g. insulin among diabetic patients.

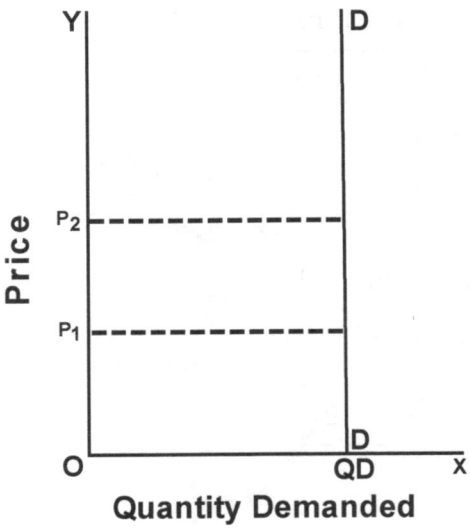

Quantity Demanded

Inelastic Demand

This occurs when a big change in price causes a small change in quantity demanded. The value ranges from 0 to 1. The price increases a lot but the demand decreases just a little bit, e.g. beer, kerosene, petrol, cigarettes, salt, etc.

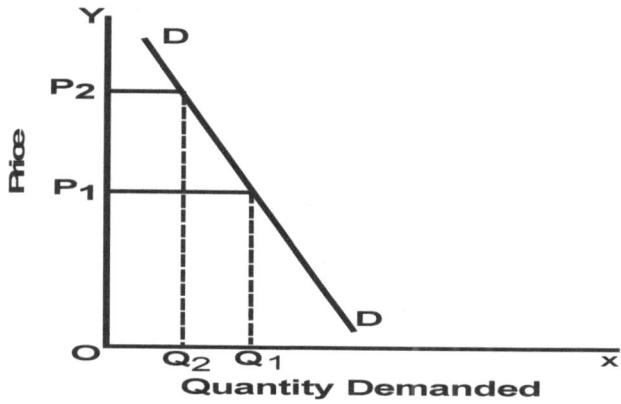

Elastic Demand

This occurs when a small change in price causes a big change in demand.

The value ranges from 1 to infinity (∞)

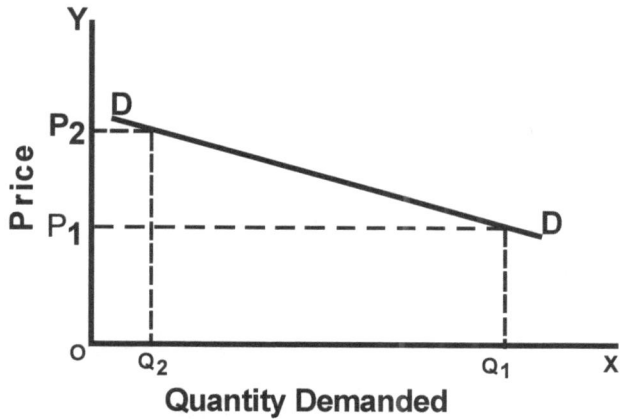

Unitary elasticity

This occurs when the price changes by 1% and the quantity demanded also changes by 1%.

The value = 1

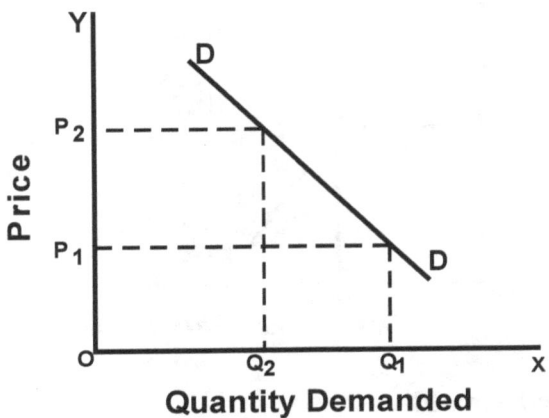

Quantity Demanded

Perfect Elasticity

This occurs when a small change in price causes an infinite change in quantity demanded.

The value = infinity (∞)

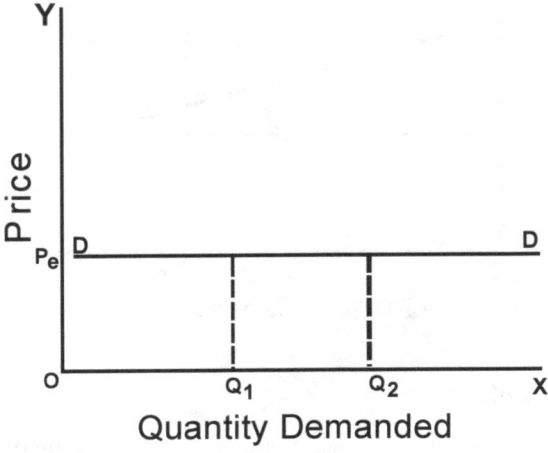

Quantity Demanded

Perfect elasticity applies to close substitutes, e.g. coffee and tea

Factors Affecting Price Elasticity of Demand

1. *Necessities of life* – For necessities of life, e.g. salt, demand is inelastic. A big increase in price causes a small decrease in demand because people will continue consuming the good

2. *Habit-forming goods* – For habit forming goods, e.g. beer, demand is inelastic. A big increase in price causes a small decrease in demand because those already addicted will continue drinking

3. *Durable goods* – Durable goods such as radios, or cars, have inelastic demand. A big decrease in price causes a small increase in demand because those who already own them will not buy extra units

4. *Time* – Immediately after the price changes, demand is inelastic, because most consumers are not aware of the price changes. As time goes by, consumers adjust to the new price and demand is elastic

5. *Availability of substitutes* – Goods that have close substitutes have elastic demand; a small increase in the price of one good causes a big decrease in demand for that good, and a high demand for the other good, as it is deemed to be cheaper

6. **The proportion of income out of the total expenditure devoted to that good** – If the proportion is very small, demand is inelastic. A big increase in price causes a small change in quantity demanded. If the proportion is big, demand is elastic, meaning that a small increase in price leads to a big decrease in demand

7. **Postponement of Consumption** - Commodities like biscuits, soft drinks, etc. whose demand is not urgent, have highly elastic demand as their consumption can be postponed in case of an increase in their prices. However, commodities with urgent demand like life -saving drugs, have inelastic demand because of their immediate

8. **Level of price** - Level of price also affects the price elasticity of demand. Costly goods like laptop, Plasma TV, etc. have highly elastic demand as their demand is very sensitive to changes in their prices. However, demand for inexpensive goods like needle, match box, etc. is inelastic as change in prices of such goods do not change their demand by a considerable amount.

9. **Income Level** - Elasticity of demand for any commodity is generally less for higher income level groups in comparison to people with low incomes. It

happens because rich people are not influenced much by changes in the price of goods. But, poor people are highly affected by increase or decrease in the price of goods. As a result, demand for lower income group is highly elastic.

Application/Importance of Price Elasticity of Demand

1. In the Determination of Output Level

For making production profitable, it is essential that the quantity of goods and services should be produced corresponding to the demand for that product. Since the changes in demand is due to the change in price, the knowledge of elasticity of demand is necessary for determining the output level.

2. In the Determination of Price

The elasticity of demand for a product is the basis of its price determination. The ratio in which the demand for a product will fall with the rise in its price and vice versa can be known with the knowledge of elasticity of demand.

If the demand for a product is inelastic, the producer can charge high price for it, whereas for an elastic demand product he will charge low price. Thus, the knowledge of elasticity of demand is essential for management in order to earn maximum profit.

3. In Price Discrimination by Monopolist

Under monopoly discrimination the problem of pricing the same commodity in two different markets also depends on the elasticity of demand in each market. In the market with elastic demand for his commodity, the discriminating monopolist fixes a low price and in the market with less elastic demand, he charges a high price.

4. In Price Determination of Factors of Production

The concept of elasticity for demand is of great importance for determining prices of various factors of production. Factors of production are paid according to their elasticity of demand. In other words, if the demand of a factor is inelastic, its price will be high and if it is elastic, its price will be low.

5. In Demand Forecasting

The elasticity of demand is the basis of demand forecasting. The knowledge of income elasticity is essential for demand forecasting of producible goods in future. Long- term production planning and management depend more on the income elasticity because management can know the effect of changing income levels on the demand for his product.

6. In Dumping

A firm enters foreign markets for dumping his product on the basis of elasticity of demand to face foreign competition.

7. In the Determination of Prices of Joint Products

The concept of the elasticity of demand is of much use in the pricing of joint products, like wool and mutton, wheat and straw, cotton and cotton seeds, etc. In such cases, separate cost of production of each product is not known.

Therefore, the price of each is fixed on the basis of its elasticity of demand. That is why products like wool, wheat and cotton having an inelastic demand are priced very high as compared to their byproducts like mutton, straw and cotton seeds which have an elastic demand.

8. In the Determination of Government Policies

The knowledge of elasticity of demand is also helpful for the government in determining its policies. Before imposing statutory price control on a product, the government must consider the elasticity of demand for that product.

The government decision to declare public utilities those industries whose products have inelastic demand and are in danger of being controlled by monopolist interests depends upon the elasticity of demand for their products.

9. Helpful in Adopting the Policy of Protection

The government considers the elasticity of demand of the products of those industries which apply for the grant of a subsidy or protection. Subsidy or protection is given to only those industries whose products have an elastic demand. As a consequence, they are unable to face foreign competition unless their prices are lowered through subsidy or by raising the prices of imported goods by imposing heavy duties on them.

10. In the Determination of Gains from International Trade

The gains from international trade depend, among others, on the elasticity of demand. A country will gain from international trade if it exports goods with less elasticity of demand and import those goods for which its demand is elastic.

In the first case, it will be in a position to charge a high price for its products and in the latter case it will be paying less for the goods obtained from the other country. Thus, it gains both ways and shall be able to increase the volume of its exports and imports.

2. Income Elasticity of Demand

This measures the extent by which the demand for a good changes due to a change in the income of consumers. It is the responsiveness of demand to a change in the income of consumers.

$$Y.E.D = \frac{\% \text{ change in Qd}}{\% \text{ change in y}}$$

$$= \frac{\text{New Qd} - \text{Old Qd} \times 100}{\text{Old Qd}} \div \frac{\text{New Y} - \text{Old Y} \times 100}{\text{Old y}}$$

Example:

Following a change in income of consumers from Kshs. 800 to Kshs. 700 per month, the quantity demanded for a good decreased from 120 to 100 units. Calculate the income elasticity of demand

$$\text{Y.E.D} = \frac{\% \text{ change in Qd}}{\% \text{ change in y}}$$

$$= \frac{\text{New Qd} - \text{Old Qd} \times 100}{\text{Old Qd}} \div \frac{\text{New Y} - \text{Old Y} \times 100}{\text{old Y}}$$

$$= \frac{100 - 120 \times 100}{120} \div \frac{700 - 800 \times 100}{120}$$

$$= -20/120 \times 100 \div -100/120 \times 100$$

$$= -16.6 \div -12.5$$

$$= 1.3$$

Interpretation

The value 1.3 means that when income decreases by 1%, quantity demanded decreases by 1.3%. Income elasticity of demand is always positive because there is a positive relationship between demand and income. As income increases, quantity demanded increases and vice versa. If the answer is negative, then the goods consumed are not normal, but inferior or Giffen goods.

3. Cross Elasticity of Demand

This measures the extent by which the quantity demanded of a good changes due to a change in the price of another related good (substitute or complementary)

$$C.E.D = \frac{\% \text{ change in Qd for good x}}{\% \text{ change in price for good y}}$$

Example 1

Following the price increase of butter from Kshs. 300 to Kshs. 400 the quantity demanded for margarine increased from 35 to 50 units. Calculate the cross elasticity of demand and state the relationship of the goods

$$C.E.D = \frac{\% \text{ change in Qd for margarine}}{\% \text{ change in price for good butter}}$$

$$= \frac{50 - 35}{35} \times 100 \quad \div \quad \frac{400 - 300}{300} \times 100$$

$$= {}^{15}/_{35} \times 100 \div {}^{100}/_{300} \times 100$$

$$= {}^{300}/_{7} \div {}^{100}/_{3}$$

$= {}^9/_7$

$= 1.3$

Interpretation

When the value is 1.3 it means that when the price of butter increases by 1% the quantity demanded of margarine increases by 1.3%.

Example 2

As a result of a price decrease for pens from Kshs. 280 to Kshs. 240 the quantity demanded of ink increased from 40 to 70 bottles. Calculate the cross elasticity and state the relationship of the goods

$$\text{C.E.D} = \frac{\text{\% change in Qd for Pen}}{\text{\% change in price for Ink}}$$

$$= \frac{70 - 40}{40} \times 100 \div \frac{240 - 280}{280} \times 100$$

$$= {}^{30}/_{40} \times 100 \div {}^{-40}/_{280} \times 100$$

$$= 87.5 \div -142$$

$$= -5.3$$

The value -5.3 means that when the price of pens decreases by 1% the quantity demanded of ink increases by 5.3%.

NB: Substitutes have a positive relationship and

complementaries have a negative relationship on elasticity of demand.

INDIFFERENCE CURVES

An indifference curve is the locus of points, each representing a different combination of two goods, but yielding the same level of utility or satisfaction. Since each combination yields the same level of utility, the consumer is indifferent between any two combinations of goods when it comes to making a choice between them. In real life a consumer can substitute one commodity for another, or make various combinations of two substitutable goods, and still get the same satisfaction. This analysis can be explained by the use of a schedule and curve

Indifference Schedule

Combinations	Commodity X	Commodity Y	Utility
A	35	6	100
B	25	8	100
C	15	12	100
D	10	22	100
E	5	31	100

Indifference Curve

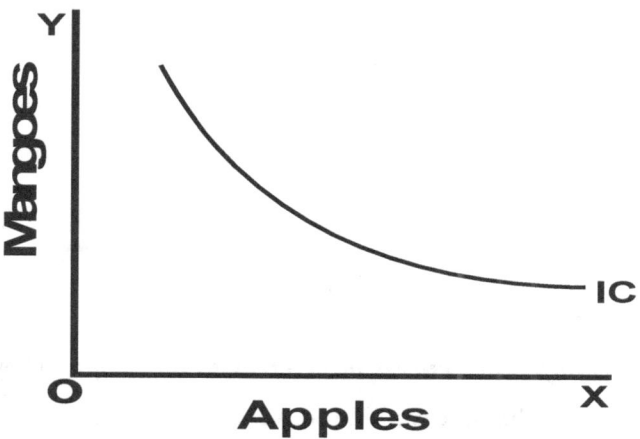

Properties of Indifference Curves

1. *Indifference curves have a negative slope*. The slope cannot be positive. The negative slope of an indifference curve means that the two commodities can be substituted for each other and that if quantity for one commodity decreases the quantity for the other must increase.

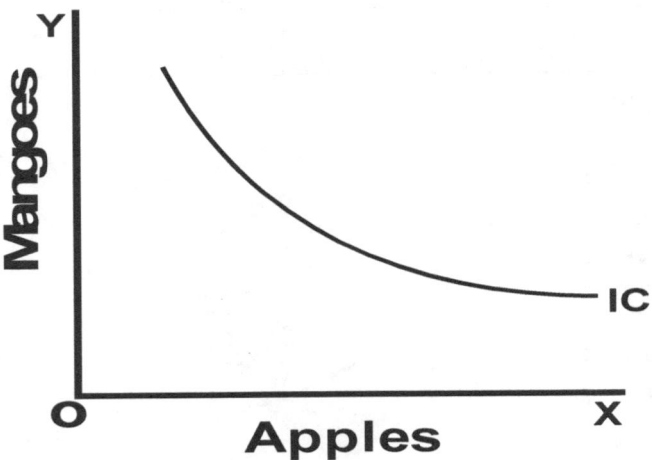

2. *Indifference curves are convex to the origin*. They cannot be concave. The convexity of the indifference curves implies that the two commodities are imperfect substitutes for each other.

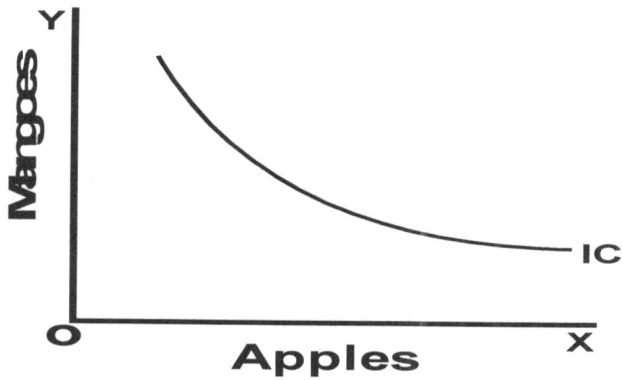

3. *Indifference curves do not intersect.* Two indifference curves can never cut each other. If two indifference curves intersect or are tangent to each other it means two different levels of satisfaction or two different combinations (one higher than the other) yielding the same level of satisfaction. One level cannot be equal to two different levels.

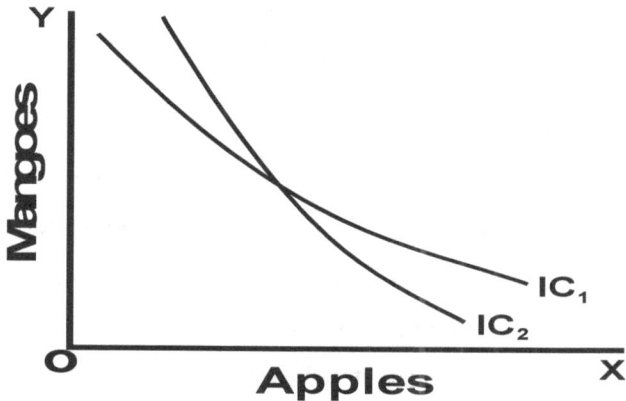

4. *A higher indifference curve indicates a higher level of satisfaction*. An indifference curve placed above and to the right of another represents a higher level of satisfaction than the lower one. This is because an upper indifference curve contains a larger quantity of one or both the goods than the lower indifference curve.

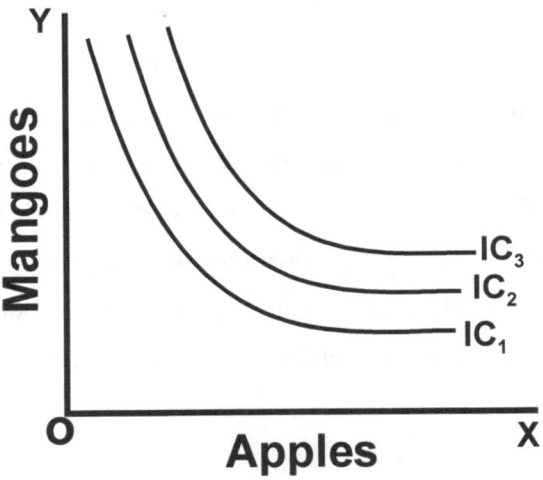

5. *Indifference curve will not touch the axis.* Another characteristic feature of indifference curve is that it will not touch the X axis or Y axis. This is born out of our assumption that the consumer is considering different combinations of two commodities. If an indifference curve touches the Y axis at a point P as shown in the figure, it means that the consumer is satisfied with OP units of y commodity and zero units

of x commodity. This is contrary to our assumption that the consumer wants both commodities although in a smaller or larger quantities. Therefore, the indifference curve will not touch either the X axis or Y axis.

Figure 4

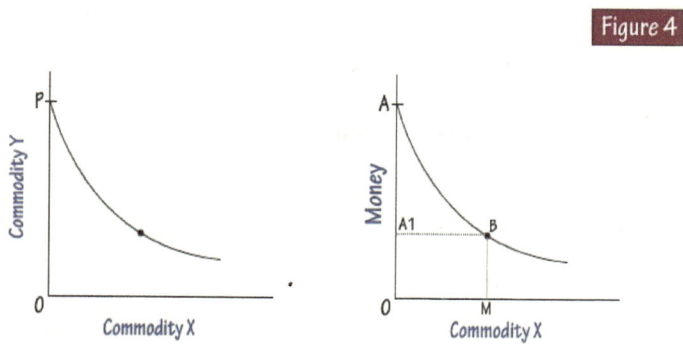

But as a special case it will touch the Y axis at point A if the combination is between Money and Commodity as shown in the Figure 4. It would then mean that the consumer either wants various combinations of money and commodity or only OA units of money which gives him command over commodity X. At point B in the figure the consumer has OM units of commodity X and OA1 units of money and this gives him the same satisfaction of having only OA units of money which means command over x and other commodities.

Applications of Indifference Curves

1. The Problem of Exchange

With the help of indifference curve technique the problem of exchange between two individuals can be discussed. We take two consumers A and B who possess two goods X and Y in fixed quantities respectively. The problem is how can they exchange the goods possessed by each other.

2. Effects of Subsidy on Consumers

The indifference curve technique can be used to measure the effects of government subsidy on low income groups. We take a situation when the subsidy is not paid in money but the consumers are supplied cereals at concessional rates, the price-difference being paid by the government. This is actually being done by the various state governments in India

3. The Problem of Rationing

The indifference curve technique is used to explain the problem arising from various systems of rationing. Usually rationing consists of giving specific and equal quantities of goods to each individual (we ignore families because equal quantities are not possible in their case). The other, rather liberal, scheme is to allow an individual more or less quantities of the rationed goods according to his taste.

4. Index Numbers: Measuring Cost of Living

The indifferent curve analysis is used in measuring the cost of living or standard of living in terms of index numbers. We come to know with the help of index numbers whether the consumer is better off or worse off by comparing two time periods when the income of the consumer and prices of two goods change.

5. The Supply of Labour

The supply curve of an individual worker can also be derived with the indifference curve technique. His offer to supply labour depends on his preference between income and leisure and on the wage rate

6. The Effect of Income Tax vs. Excise Duty

The indifference curve technique helps in considering the welfare implications of income tax vs. excise duty or sales tax. Whether an income tax hurts the tax payer more or an excise duty of an equal amount? Let us take a taxpayer who is required to pay, say Rs. 4000 annually either as income tax or as excise tax on a commodity X. It is further assumed that he will continue to buy the commodity even after the imposition of the duty when its price goes up.

7. The Saving Plan of an Individual

The indifference curve technique can also be used to study the saving plan of an individual. An individual's decision to save depends upon his present and future income, his tastes and preferences for present and future commodities, their expected prices, on the current and future rate of interest, and on the stock of his savings.

CHAPTER THREE

SUPPLY ANALYSIS

SUPPLY

Supply is the amount of products that producers are willing and able to supply in the market at a given market price. It is assumed that any producer aims at maximizing profits.

Law of Supply

This states that 'ceteris paribus' (holding all other factors constant) as the price increases, supply also increases and vice versa. At higher prices, producers want to supply more so as to make a lot of profits. The law of supply can be explained by the use of a supply schedule and supply curve.

Supply Schedule

This is a table showing quantities of goods supplied at different market prices:

Supply of eggs per week

Price per egg (Ksh.	Quantity supplied (No. of eggs)
5	10
10	20
15	40
30	80

Supply Curve

This is a graph showing quantities of goods supplied at different market prices:

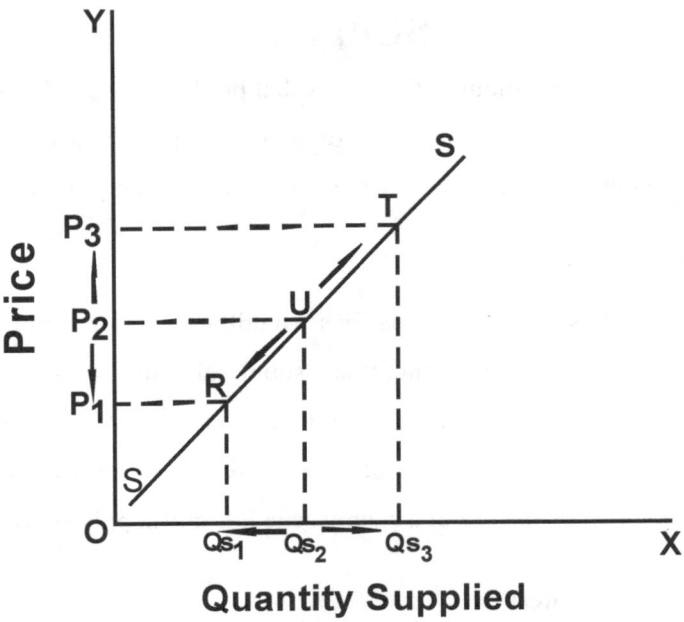

Quantity Supplied

The supply curve is upward sloping from the left to the right, showing a positive relationship between the quantity supplied and the price. As the price increases, quantity supplied increases and vice versa.

Factors Affecting Supply

1. ***Cost of Production*** – The price of inputs, e.g. land, labour, etc. determine the cost of production. When

the cost of production increases, the level of profits decreases and some producers can't afford to produce; thus production decreases and supply also decreases

2. ***The price of the good in question*** – When the price of the goods increases, the producers will make more profit and this encourages them to produce more, and supply increases, and vice versa

3. ***State of technology*** – With improved technology, it implies that with the same amount of resources, production is faster and more efficient; hence supply increases and vice versa

4. ***Number of producers*** – As the number of producers increases, supply also increases and vice versa

5. ***Weather conditions*** – Poor weather conditions like drought discourage production and therefore supply decreases and vice versa

6. ***Profit level of producers*** – As the income (profits) level of producers increases, it means they can afford many factors of production and therefore production and supply increase and vice versa

7. ***Political situation in the country*** – Wars discourage investment or destroy existing investments. Production and supply decrease as a result

8. ***Government policy*** – Taxes on inputs or products increase the cost of production and the level of profits

decreases. This reduces production and hence supply. The Government can also restrict production of some commodities, e.g. plastic bags

9. *Time and seasons* – Some products require time to be produced or grow and that is why we have seasons of plenty and seasons of scarcity

10. *The price of other related goods* – Assume that maize and bananas can be produced with the same technology. If the price of bananas increases while that of maize remains the same, most producers will switch to the production of bananas. This will increase the supply of bananas and reduce the supply of maize (uprooting of some cash crops)

11. *The objective of the producer* – If the objective of the producer is to make profits, then supply depends on the level of profit. On the other hand, if the objective is not to make profit, then supply increases even if the profits are low

A Movement along the Supply Curve

This is caused by changes in the price of the good, which in turn causes a change in quantity supplied. A movement along the supply curve means a movement of quantity supplied points along the same supply curve.

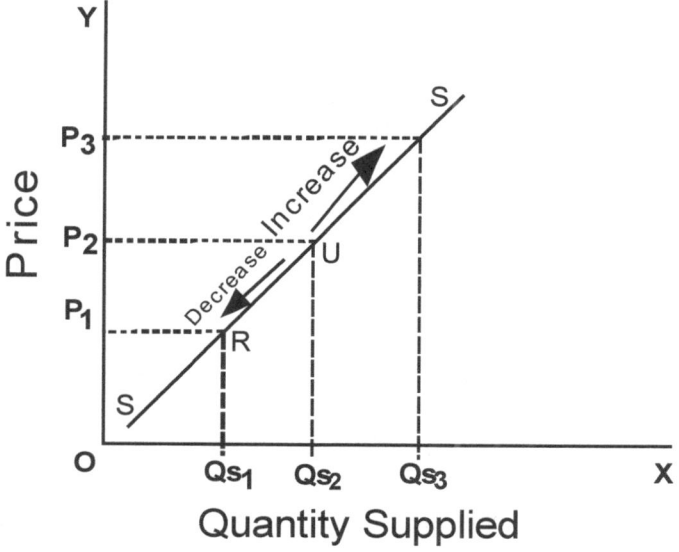

This is also known as change in quantity supplied. When prices increase from P2 to P3 the quantity supplied increases from QS2 to QS3 and this leads to a movement from point U to T along the same supply curve. When the price decreases from P2 to P1 the quantity supplied decreases from QS2 to QS1 and this leads to a movement from point U to R along the same supply curve.

A Shift of the Supply Curve

When determinants of supply other than the price of the good change (e.g. technology) there is a shift of the supply curve. It can shift to the right or left depending on the changes. This is also known as change in supply

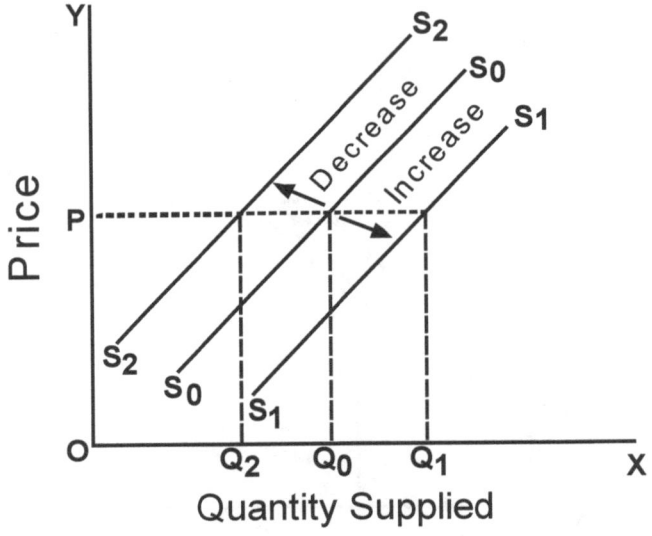

Assume that S0 is the original supply curve. When the determinants of supply change against the commodity (e.g. poor weather conditions like drought), supply decreases from Q0 to Q2. A decrease in supply causes the whole supply curve to shift upwards to the left from S0 to S2. An increase in supply causes the supply curve to shift downwards to the right from S0 to S1 because the determinants of supply are favourable and therefore quantity supplied increases from Q0 to Q1.

Price Elasticity of Supply

This refers to the responsiveness of supply due to a change in the price of a good

$$\text{P.E.S.} = \frac{\%\ \text{change in QS}}{\%\ \text{change in price}}$$

$$= \frac{\text{New Qs} - \text{Old Qs}}{\text{Old Qs}} \times 100 \div \frac{\text{New P} - \text{Old P}}{\text{Old P}} \times 100$$

Example

Following a price increase in bananas from Kshs. 6 to Kshs. 8 per banana, the quantity supplied increased from 65 to75 bananas per day. Calculate the price elasticity of supply

$$\text{P.E.S} = \frac{\%\ \text{change in QS}}{\%\ \text{change in price}}$$

$$= \frac{\text{New Qs} - \text{Old Q s}}{\text{Old Qs}} \times 100 \div \frac{\text{New P} - \text{Old P}}{\text{old P}} \times 100$$

$$= \frac{75 - 65}{65} \times 100 \div \frac{8 - 6}{6} \times 100$$

$$= {}^{10}/_{65} \times 100 \div {}^{2}/_{6} \times 100$$

$$= {}^{200}/_{13} \div {}^{100}/_{3}$$

$= {}^{200}/_{13} \text{ X } {}^{3}/_{100}$

$= {}^{6}/_{13}$

$= 0.5$

Interpretation

The value 0.5 means that when the price of bananas increases by 1%, quantity supplied increases by 0.5%. Price elasticity of supply is always positive because there is a positive relationship between quantity supplied and the price. As the price increases, supply also increases and vice versa.

Degrees or Categories of Price Elasticity of Supply

Depending on the value obtained, we have various categories of price elasticity of supply:

Perfectly Inelastic Supply

This occurs when a change in price does not cause any change in supply. The value is equal to 0. Supply is the same at all prices, e.g. insulin among diabetic patients

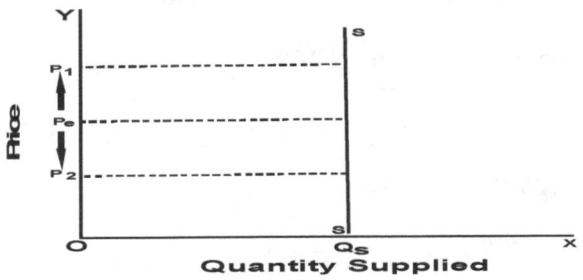

Inelastic Supply

This occurs when a big change in prices causes a small change in quantity supplied. The price increases a lot but the supply increases just a little bit, e.g. petrol and beer. The value ranges from 0 to 1

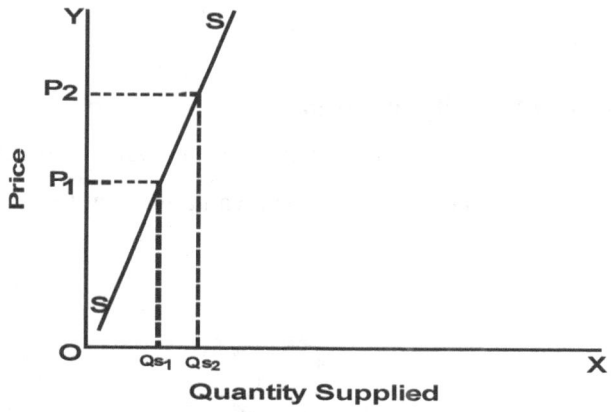

Elastic Supply

This occurs when a small change in price causes a big change in quantity supplied. The value ranges from 1 to infinity (∞)

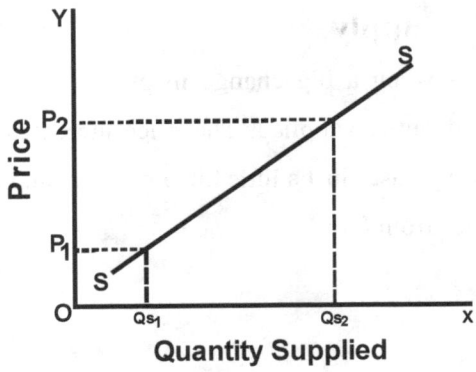

Quantity Supplied

Unitary elasticity of supply

This occurs when the price changes by 1% and the quantity supplied also changes by 1%. The value is equal to 1

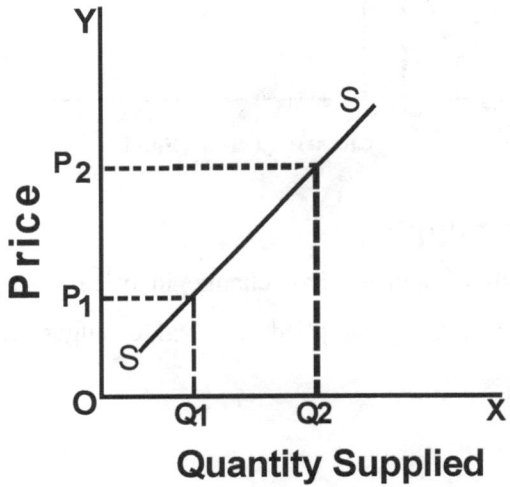

Quantity Supplied

Perfectly elasticity of supply

This occurs when a small change in prices causes an infinite change in quantity supplied. The value is equal to infinity (∞). It applies to all substitute goods, e.g. tea and coffee

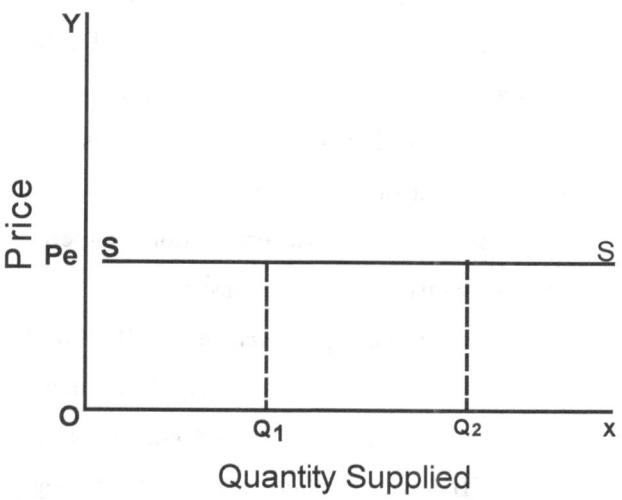

Quantity Supplied

Factors Affecting Price Elasticity of Supply

1. *Cost of production* - Goods that are very expensive to produce have inelastic supply. A big increase in price of the good causes a small increase in quantity supplied, because most producers cannot afford to increase production

2. *Method of production* - Goods that require complex methods of production have inelastic supply because an increase in price causes a small change in supply,

as many producers cannot manage to produce more. Supply is elastic if the method of production is simple

3. *Nature of commodity* - Goods that are perishable, e.g. tomatoes, have inelastic supply. A big decrease in price causes a small decrease in quantity supplied, because producers will continually supply them; they cannot be stored for a long time to be sold in future

4. *Existence of excess capacity* - If there is excess capacity, supply is elastic; a small increase in price would cause a big increase in quantity supplied as there is room to increase production. If there is no excess capacity, supply is inelastic

5. *Conditions under production* - If supply is controlled by the Government supply is inelastic; a big change in price causes a small change in quantity supplied. If it is controlled by a cartel then supply is elastic; a small change in price will cause a big change in quantity supplied

6. *Availability of factors of production* - Supply is elastic due to the price of a product. If factors of production are easily available it is elastic and if factors of production are not readily available it is inelastic

7. *Law of returns* - If the product is produced under increasing returns to scale then a small increase in price causes a big increase in supply and hence

supply is elastic. Supply is inelastic if production is under decreasing or negative returns to scale

8. **Risk-Taking:** The willingness of entrepreneurs to take risks also affects price elasticity of supply. This, in its turn, depends on the system of incentives and disincentives. If, for example, the marginal rates of tax are very high, a price rise will not evoke much response among producers.

9. **The Definition of the Commodity** - As in the case of demand, elasticity of supply also depends on the definition of the commodity. The narrowly a commodity is defined, the greater its elasticity of supply. For example, it is easier for a tailor to transfer resources from producing red skirts to green skirts than from skirts to men's trousers.

10. **Time** - Time also exerts considerable influence on the elasticity of supply. Supply is more elastic in the long run than in the short run. The reason is easy to find out. The longer the time period the easier it is to shift resources among products, following a change in their relative prices.

11. **Factor Mobility** - The ease with which factors of production can be moved from one use to another will affect price elasticity of supply. The higher the mobility of factor services, the greater will be elasticity

Importance (Application) of Price Elasticity of Supply

1. It helps consumers in planning their purchases; e.g. they will buy and keep goods to avoid future shortages if supply is elastic due to price decrease
2. It helps producers in planning production; i.e. they may increase supply when the price increases if supply is elastic
3. It helps the Government in controlling/regulating production; e.g. through price control where supply is elastic when the price decreases

DETERMINATION OF MARKET PRICE

In a perfect competitive market where we have many buyers and sellers, the market price is determined by the market forces of *demand* and *supply*. The market price is determined at a point where the demand and supply curves meet

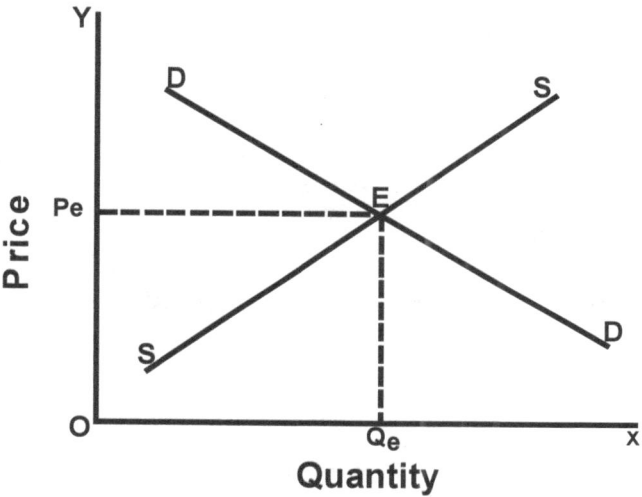

E = Equilibrium point where the demand and supply curves meet.

Pe = Market equilibrium price.

Qe = Equilibrium quantity where Qs = Qd.

At equilibrium, buyers are willing and able to buy Qe and sellers are willing and able to sell at Pe, i.e. equilibrium market price

Any price other than the equilibrium price Pe causes disequilibrium in the market, which may lead to either excess supply or excess demand

Excess Supply

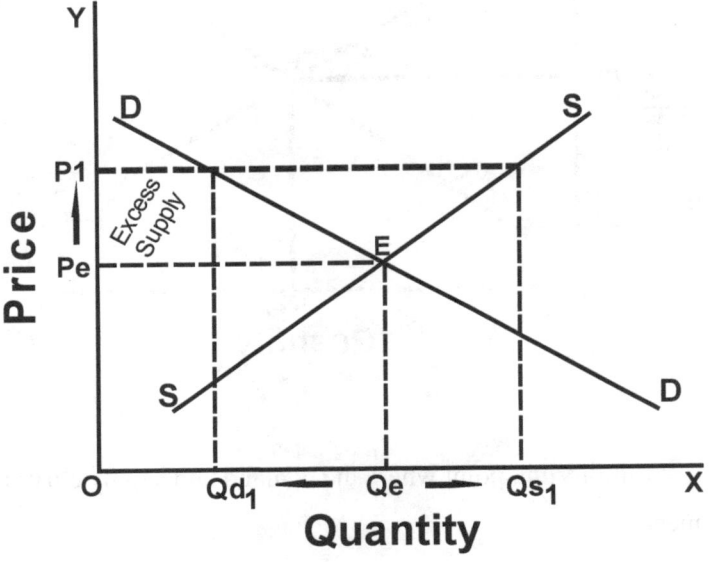

When the price increases from Pe to P1 the quantity demanded decreases from Qe to Qd1 and supply increases from Qe to Qs1. At a higher price than Pe, supply is greater than demand and this causes excess supply given by Qs1-Qd1. Due to excess supply, prices will start to fall until the equilibrium price Pe is reached.

Excess Demand

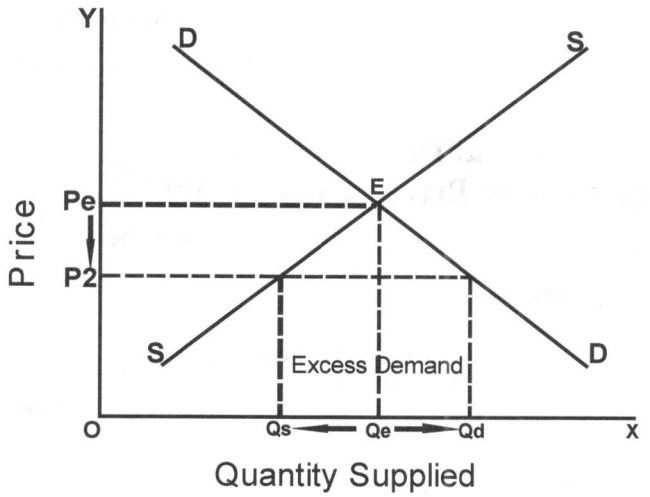

When the price decreases from Pe to P2 the quantity demanded increases from Qe to Qd, whereas supply decreases from Qe to Qs. Demand is greater than supply (calculated by Qd-Qs to get the excess demand). This may lead to shortage of goods. Due to a shortage of goods, price may start to increase until Pe is reached.

Other Methods of Price Determination

1. *Bargaining/haggling* – Prices of some commodities are arrived at after bargaining

2. *Price control* – This is where prices of some commodities are fixed by the Government, especially

for public utilities

3. *Auction* – This is where buyers suggest the price of the products. The buyer who offers the highest price (highest bidder) becomes the buyer of the product

Mathematical Determination of Equilibrium Price and Quantity

Given Qd =100 - 2p (demand curve) and Qs = 4 + 4p (supply curve)

Calculate the equilibrium price and quantity

Solution

At equilibrium Qs = Qd

= 4 + 4P = 100 - 2P

4P + 2P = 100 - 4

6p = 96

P = 96/6

P= 16

QS: = 4 + 4PQd: 100 - 2P

= 4+4 (16)= 100 - 2 (16)

= 4 + 64= 100 - 32

Qs = 68Qd = 68

Disequilibrium

This occurs when the demand is not equal to supply. Either the demand exceeds the supply or the supply exceeds the demand

Causes of market disequilibrium

1. Government intervention
2. Nature of commodity
3. Anticipation of price changes
4. Seasonal changes
5. Uncontrolled population growth
6. Trade unions
7. Hoarding practices

Price Control

This is where the Government fixes the prices of essential goods.

Objectives of price control

1. To protect consumers against being exploited by greedy producers who may overcharge
2. To protect producers against being exploited by middlemen or agents who may offer low prices
3. To ensure that producers have stable income by ensuring that prices of goods don't fluctuate too much

4. To eliminate monopolies which may exploit the public by overcharging
5. To help bridge the gap between different income groups in society
6. To ration scarce resources to ensure that everybody gets a share

The Government can fix prices above or below the market equilibrium price

Maximum Price/Price Ceiling

This is the price fixed by the Government below the equilibrium price. *Maximum price* is the price above which sellers cannot sell and buyers cannot buy the products

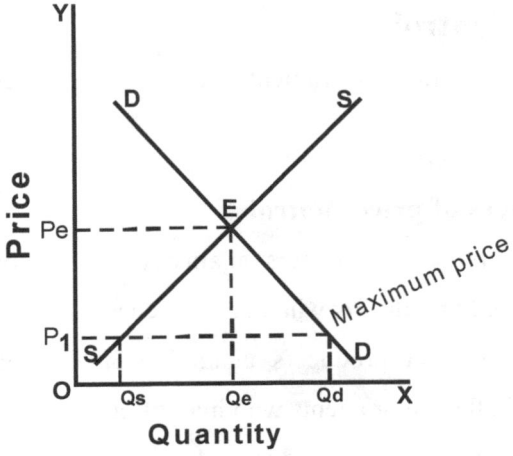

Effects of maximum price

1. It leads to excess demand and hence a shortage of goods
2. It leads to low production of goods because producers are not making profit
3. Low production may lead to closing down of industries
4. Closing down of industries may lead to unemployment in the economy
5. Producers may prefer to sell their products abroad where prices are high, and this causes a shortage of goods at home
6. It may lead to the emergence of a black market, i.e. producers not selling at Government price and selling the product to relatives and friends
7. It may lead to wastage of time, as witnessed in long queues when people are waiting for goods that are in short supply
8. Excess consumption may force the Government to ration the consumption of goods to ensure that everybody gets a share

Minimum Price/Price Floor

This price is fixed by the Government above the market equilibrium price. *Minimum price* is the price below which sellers cannot sell and buyers cannot buy the product

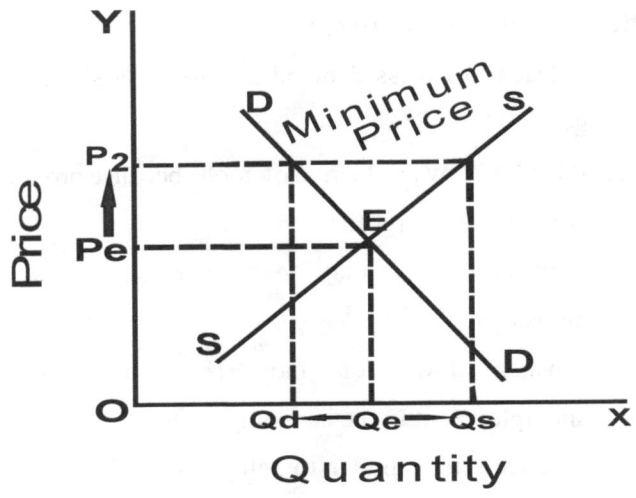

Effects of minimum price

1. It leads to low demand for goods and services and hence supply decreases
2. It may lead to excess supply hence wastage of resources
3. Low demand leads to low production
4. Low production leads to closing down of some industries
5. Closing down of industries will lead to unemployment
6. Unemployment promotes poverty in the country

CHAPTER FOUR

PRODUCTION

MEANING

Production is the process of converting inputs into outputs. It is the process of creating goods and services to satisfy human wants. It is the increase of utility to goods and services to satisfy human wants. It is assumed that any producer aims at maximizing profits. Production is the transformation of inputs into output. In economics it means the creation of goods and services which have exchange value. This means that it is an activity which results in the creation of economic goods and services. Production also means the creation of utility (satisfaction). It covers the following activities:

1. Transforming raw materials to finished products
2. Distribution of goods from a factory to a retail shop
3. Holding stocks of goods until required (warehousing)
4. Provision of some services such as retailing, banking, insurance, entertainment etc.

There are two types of goods, i.e. producer goods and consumer goods. Producer goods are goods that are used to produce other goods, e.g. raw materials, machines, etc.

Consumer goods are goods that are consumed directly by consumers, e.g. bread, soda, etc.

Importance of Production

1. The purpose of production is to satisfy human wants. People engage in production in order to earn the means by which they can satisfy their own wants and those of others

2. Production increases the economic welfare of the people by raising their standards of living and enabling them to satisfy more fully a greater number of their wants

3. It leads to efficient and effective use of resources

4. It leads to increased employment

5. It leads to economic growth and development

Factors of Production and Their Rewards

These are the things that are needed in the production process, without which production cannot take place. They are goods and services used as inputs in the production process. They aid production and therefore are indispensable in any process of production. They are sometimes known as:

1. Factors/inputs

2. Production resources

3. Agents of production

4. Inputs

Their quality and availability determines the total volume of production. The main factors of production are:

1. Land

2. Labour

3. Capital

4. Entrepreneurship (Management)

Land

Land consists of all natural resources found above and below the earth's surface. Land is the source of all raw materials, e.g. minerals, soil, wildlife, etc. It is a gift of nature or natural resources. It is the main factor on which all production depends, as it provides the space where all production is undertaken. It may be fixed in quantity in the short-run, but in the long-run, the quantity of land can be increased through reclamation or change of use. It is immobile geographically, but its use can be changed and so it has mobility from this point of view. Land is permanent, though it can be wasted. Productivity of land can be increased by using greater units of labour and capital. The reward for land as a factor of production is *rent*.

Labour

Labour includes all those activities, mental or physical,

undertaken by man for some monetary consideration. It does not include any work done for leisure or which does not carry any monetary reward. Its supply depends on population size and structure, education and training, nutrition, health and other social and cultural factors. Its quality determines the social and economic development of organizations or countries. It is rewarded in the form of *wages, salaries, fee or commission.*

Capital

Capital comprises all manmade resources used in the production process. It comprises all wealth, other than land, which is used for further production of wealth. It increases the productivity of labour and land. Its formation depends on savings and investment. There are two types of capital: physical and human capital. Physical capital includes tools, machinery, raw materials, buildings, roads, railways, etc. Human capital is the acquired skills and capacities of the people. Human capital is regarded as more important than physical capital in production. The reward for capital is *interest.*

Entrepreneurship

For production to take place, somebody needs to bring the factors of production together, organize, and combine them in the right proportions. This is called organization, which is the work of an entrepreneur. The main functions of an entrepreneur include:

i. Providing money to start up the business

ii. Employing the services of land

iii. Responsibility for the day-to-day running of the business

iv. Innovating and undertaking all risks, e.g. fire, theft etc.

v. Selling the products of the undertaking

vi. Rewarding the other factors of production

vii. Taking responsibility for profit or loss

Since the entrepreneur is the one who gets what remains after all the other factors have been paid, he is sometimes called the residual claimant of production. The reward for entrepreneurship is **profit or loss**; profit for good management and loss for mismanagement.

Ricardian Theory of Rent

This is one of the main theories of rent. Ricardo defined rent as the portion of the produce of land which is paid to the landlord for the use of the original and indestructible powers of land. In popular language, the term rent is applied to whatever is usually paid by a tenant to his landlord. Economic rent, according to Ricardo, is the true surplus left after the expenses of cultivation – as represented by payment to labour, capital and enterprise – have been met. According to this theory, marginal lands yield no rent, while more fertile land yields greater return. Hence according to Ricardo, rent arose from the natural variation in the fertility of land.

The theory, therefore, outlined the following guidelines for determining rent:

1. Land which was just worthwhile to cultivate (marginal land) yielded no rent
2. The more fertile the land, the greater the rent yielded
3. The value of the produce in excess of the product yielded by the marginal land determined the rent

In summary, the theory has two elements:

i. Rent arises because certain lands are more fertile compared to others; in this way surplus production occurs due to the difference in the fertility of land

ii. Land is scarce and rent arises due to scarcity of land. According to Ricardo, more fertile lands will pay more rent because they are scarcer

Criticism of the Theory

1. There is no original and indestructible power of the soil. Fertile soils, after being constantly cultivated, lose their fertility to a large extent. The fertility of land depends upon natural circumstances like

climate, nature of the soil etc. These circumstances are likely to change

2. It is also objected that Ricardo has used the term fertility of land in a vague manner

3. According to this theory, rent arises due to differences in the fertility of land. But it has been pointed out that even if all the land were equally fertile, rent will still arise because when more and more units of labour and capital are applied, then due to the law of diminishing returns, marginal productivity will tend to diminish

4. According to Ricardo, no-rent land always exists but this is not correct. In certain cases all lands may have some surplus production over cost of production

5. The theory considers land as fixed in supply. Land is fixed in the absolute sense, but large areas of land have alternative uses. The area of land can also be increased through reclamation

6. Productivity of land does not depend entirely on fertility. Position, investment and effective use of capital are also significance in determining levels of productivity

DIVISION OF LABOUR AND SPECIALIZATION

This is an important characteristic of modern production. There is hardly any production unit of a respectable size which does not organize production in specialized units. This is sometimes called specialization. Division of labour or specialization is a strategic component of most productive enterprises and is seen as the key determinant of efficiency and competitiveness.

Division of labour is defined as the splitting of tasks into various smaller units and entrusting each unit to particular individuals or groups of workers for execution, depending on their areas of expertise, skills and experience. In this way a small part of the work is undertaken by one person and the whole job is completed by different labourers. For example, a car is manufactured by different workers and one worker is responsible for one part only.

However division of labour can be distinguished from specialization in that division of labour entails dividing the job of producing a particular product into many individual tasks and training different people to complete each task, while specialization refers to concentrating labour on a particular task to increase productive efficiency.

Types of Division of Labour

1. ***Complicated/Process Division of Labour***: This is the case where one job is subdivided into different parts and each part is given to a separate set of workers. For example, in the textile industry, we have spinning, weaving and dyeing, each being performed by different people, but ending up with a finished product, i.e. cloth

2. ***Occupational/Professional Division of Labour***: This is the case where different people adopt different occupations; e.g. doctors, engineers, economists, lawyers etc. have different occupations

3. ***Geographical/Territorial/International Division of Labour***: This is where different geographical regions or countries have specialized in the production of different goods and services. It is based on differences in soils, climate, skills and cost of production. It is the basis of international trade

Advantages of Division of Labour

1. ***Promotes Efficiency***: Labour efficiency improves when tasks are divided into specialized units and assigned to individuals with specific skills in those areas. This is because workers are specialized in these areas and they will be able to produce more and higher quality output

2. ***Reduced supervision***: This contributes to the reduction in administrative costs essentials for an organization, in that workers are easily supervised when they have been assigned specific tasks, which they are directly accountable for; each member of staff therefore takes the initiative to perform to his/her fullest capability due to accountability and this increases productivity

3. ***Responsibility***: With accountability in place, workers develop a sense of responsibility towards their tasks, which enhances their productivity. Motivation is then created within workers and their performance improves

4. ***Easy Management***: With division of labour, management of the organization becomes easier. This is because work is divided into specialized tasks, making it easier for the management to trace areas of fault and find corrective measures. This enhances effectiveness and efficiency in production

5. ***Specialization***: Specialization is increased with division of labour as given individuals repeatedly do their tasks. This may lead to innovations in the tasks which they know best. In other words, workers may be encouraged to innovate better ways of performing their tasks, which would improve their productivity and efficiency

6. ***Increased Output***: Division of labour leads to increase in output, since workers are specialized in the tasks they know best. This enables the firm to enjoy the advantages of large-scale production, i.e., economies of scale both internally and externally. With this in place production costs will decrease, with an increase in efficiency and productivity

7. ***Reduction in Costs***: Division of labour promotes cost-effectiveness; workers become efficient and thereby perform their given tasks at minimum costs. With the economies of large scale enjoyed and the limitation of functional overlaps, low-cost production improves

8. ***Time Saving***: Division of labour reduces time-wasting; workers know their tasks and can therefore perform them in a shorter time period, thereby reducing the overall time taken to realize a given level of output

9. ***Employment Creation***: When work is divided into different occupations there is a chance that most people will find employment appropriate to their talents. Division of labour, therefore, increases the number and diversity of jobs

10. ***Increase in Skills***: Workers acquire greater skill at their jobs. By reducing the workers' business to a

single operation it necessarily increases skills through repetitive performance

11. *Less Fatigue*: It is believed that a worker habituated to the repetition of simple tasks becomes less fatigued by their tasks

12. *Promotes International Trade*: Due to large scale production the excess products are exported, encouraging trade between nations

13. *Encourages Teamwork*: The different sections depend on each other to have the final finished product and thus teamwork is emphasized

Disadvantages of Division of Labour

1. *Monotony*: Division of labour leads to monotony in work; an individual is made to perform a given task repeatedly through the working period without a change. This makes the work monotonous

2. *Demotivation*: Division of labour demotivates an individual and may retard human development due to the worker's inability to diversify. Performance of the same task throughout the working period may also be demotivating since there are no challenges

3. *Over-specialization*: With division of labour workers specialize only in specific areas. This limits their ability to move to other occupations and also increases their chances of remaining unemployed in

the event that they resign or are dismissed from previous employment

4. ***Increased cost of production***: Workers who are specialized in certain tasks may wish to command higher wages or rewards for their labour services, which the management may have no choice but to offer so as to retain them. This may increase the cost of production in the event that the higher wage paid is not accompanied by higher productivity and efficiency on the part of the worker

5. ***Case of Absenteeism***: The organization may incur significant costs if the workers are absent for one reason or another. This is because there is a possibility of production stalling for a given period and/or an abrupt labour separation, which may be very costly to an organization

6. ***Case of Minimum Supervision***: Some workers may take advantage of the minimum supervision present and make division of labour counterproductive

7. ***Increased Fatigue***:Under division of labour, it is necessary for all workers to maintain the same pace so as to reduce the fatigue of the slower workers. Fatigue may be increased by the effort required to keep pace with the quicker workers

8. ***High degree of interdependence***: If production is disrupted in one part of a factory, work in other parts

will also be affected

9. *Lack of identity*: It may be difficult for the workers to identify themselves with the finished products since many people are involved in producing that product. Hence workers have little pride in the job and become alienated

10. *Reduces mobility of labour*: The more specialized the workforce becomes, the less occupationally mobile it is

11. *Division of labour leads to standardization and use of machinery*: This has led to the disappearance of traditional crafts, thus turning labour into being just a machine attendant.

Limits of Division of Labour

Specialization and division of labour are not processes that can be applied indefinitely without limitations. Work cannot usually be broken down into smaller and smaller parts forever. Division of labour is limited by the following factors:

1. *The extent of the market*: Division of labour is associated with large-scale production that requires a relatively large market

2. *The extent to which exchange and distribution networks are developed*: Transport and banking systems are necessary if the products of division of

labour are to be exchanged effectively

3. ***Nature of goods and services***: Some good and services, by their very nature, cannot be produced by division of labour processes

4. ***The size of the labour force:*** If there are only one or two workers then division of labour is not possible. It is only possible where the workforce is large.

Firm and Industry

When the four factors of production are combined for the purpose of producing goods and services, a business *unit/firm* is created. A firm is small in size, has one point of management and usually produces a single product. A group of firms forms an industry. An industry is large in size, produces many products and has more than one point of management.

Objectives of a Firm/Business

1. To maximize profits
2. To maximize sales
3. To maximize sales revenues
4. To control the market
5. To eliminate competitors from the market
6. To survive in business

Localisation and Delocalisation of Industry

Localisation is the concentration of a certain industry in a particular area or region. It is related to specialization by areas or regions. Delocalisation means the spreading of a particular industry. There are various factors that are considered when locating an industry, and these are:

1. Nearness to the targeted market
2. Availability of raw materials
3. Security
4. Good transport facilities
5. Government policy
6. Climatic and weather conditions
7. Cost of land
8. Room for expansion
9. Availability of labour
10. Availability of water and electricity

Factors that limit industrialization

1. Insecurity
2. Lack of raw materials
3. Lack of market for finished goods
4. Stiff competition from developed countries
5. Poor transport and communication network
6. Lack of modern technology
7. Lack of capital
8. Lack of managerial skills

9. Lack of skilled labour

10.Lack of land for expansion

Policy measures to promote Industrialization

1. Improve infrastructure

2. Licensing

3. Training

4. Advertising/promotions

5. Legislation

6. Providing security

7. Subsidies

8. Providing fair competition

9. Price control

10.Financial support

Types of Businesses

There are two major types of businesses:

a) Small scale business

b) Large scale business

Small Scale Businesses

Features

1. They have limited capital

2. They employ few workers

3. They have a small market

4. They make smaller profits/losses
5. Formation is easy as they require less initial capital and face fewer legal requirements
6. They are established on small parcels of land
7. They produce small outputs

Advantages of small scale businesses

1. They provide credit facilities
2. They have personal contacts with customers
3. Most of them are located near the customer
4. They operate for long hours and almost daily
5. It requires small initial capital which is easy to raise
6. There are low running costs, e.g. wages, advertising, etc.
7. They create employment for the owner
8. Formation is simple as they face few legal formalities
9. They are easy to manage
10. They are flexible as they can be changed from one form to another
11. Decision making is fast

Disadvantages of small scale businesses

1. They do not enjoy economies of scale that may occur due bulk buying
2. They do not make a lot of profits
3. They cannot employ qualified personnel

4. They do not have capital for advertising so as to increase sales
5. They cannot bear risks
6. They cannot make use of machinery and modern technology

Large Scale Businesses

Features

1. They have a lot of capital
2. They have large market size
3. They produce large output
4. They employ many workers
5. They make high profits/losses
6. They are established on large parcels of land
7. Formation is complex since they face more legal formalities and require more capital

Advantages of large scale businesses

1. They operate on a large scale and hence enjoy *economies of scale*, e.g. they can obtain bank loans or can get discounts
2. They make a lot of profits
3. They can employ qualified workers who provide quality services
4. They have enough capital for advertising, leading to increased sales and profit

5. They can bear risks
6. They can use machinery and modern technology

Disadvantages

1. They have poor personal contact with customers
2. They incur high running costs
3. Decision making is slow
4. They do not provide credit facilities to customers
5. They are often located in towns far away from the customers
6. They are not flexible in terms of operations as they cannot be changed from one form to another

How Small Firms Grow Large

Internal growth or Organic growth

This is where firms grow internally by the use of savings, profits, loans, etc.

Internal growth is a slow form of growth.

External growth

This can be done through combinations, amalgamations or integration.

Integration is done in two ways;

i. **Takeover** – This is when a firm buys shares of another firm and takes it over completely; e.g. in

2002, Kenya Breweries took over Castle Breweries

ii. **Merger** – This occurs when two or more friendly firms combine and operate as one, e.g. Kenol/Kobil or GlaxoSmithklineBeacham

Lines of Integration

1. **Vertical Integration.** This occurs when two or more firms in the same industry at different level of production combine, e.g. a wheat firm combines with a bakery

2. **Horizontal Integration.** This occurs when two or more firms in the same industry, at the same level of production, combine, e.g. Amy's salon and Liz's salon

3. **Conglomerate.** This occurs when two or more firms in different industries, at different levels of production, combine, e.g. bank, hospital, bakery, hotel, bar, car wash, salon, etc.

Why Firms Want to Grow Large

1. To make more profits
2. To enjoy economies of scale
3. To improve their financial position
4. To control market share
5. Intrinsic value; some owners find satisfaction and pride when they see their businesses grow large

TYPES OF BUSINESS UNITS

Sole Proprietor

This is a one-person business and is the most common and also the oldest type of business. Formation is simple. It is a small-scale business employing very few people. A single person provides the capital, takes decisions and bears the risks of the enterprise. He carries all the functions of an entrepreneur. He takes the profits or loses. It has a limited life as it can end at any time.

Advantages
1. Small capital needed to start
2. Increased efficiency because the owner must work hard
3. Independence; there is no consultation. This can lead to quick decisions
4. Little resource wastage due to personal supervision
5. Personal contact with both customers and employees
6. Private accounts that are not revealed to any other person

Disadvantages
1. Long hours of working
2. If the owner is sick the business may collapse
3. Less finances, which limits the expansion of the business

4. Lack of specialization; the owner does everything
5. Lack of continuity in case of death
6. Unlimited liability; there is no legal distinction between the owner and his business
7. Inability to undertake research due to limited finances

Partnership

A partnership is a proprietorship with more than one proprietor. When two or more people agree to share the responsibility for a business they form a partnership. The capital is contributed by the partners. Partnership is governed by a deed and there is consultation. They are voluntarily formed by individuals to earn profits. They are formed by two (2) or up to a maximum of twenty (20) partners. There is no formal legal process required to start such a business but they are based on agreements signed by all the partners. The partners share the responsibilities of running the business, although one need not be actively involved. Each partner is both jointly and separately liable as there is no limit to liability. Like sole proprietorship, partnership has a limited life in that it can be ended at any time due to the death, withdrawal, bankruptcy or incapacitation of any one member.

There are two types of partnerships;

Ordinary Partnership – All partners are responsible for the debts incurred. All members have unlimited liability

Limited Liability – The liability of the members is restricted to the amount of capital they have put into the business. However, there must be at least one member with unlimited liability. Limited partners do not participate in the management of the firm

There are various types of partners:

1. Active partner – They are also known as acting or working partners and they are responsible for the day-to-day running of the business
2. Sleeping partner – They are also known as dormant partners or financing partners. They do not participate in the management of the business
3. Minor partner – This is one who has not attained the age of majority but enjoys the benefits of the partnership
4. Major partner – This is one who is over 18 years and is liable for all the debts incurred by the company
5. New partner – This is one who enters into an existing partnership with the consent of all the members
6. Outgoing partner – This is one who retires from the partnership with the consent of all the members, or in accordance with the initial agreement

Advantages of Partnership

1. Easy and less costly to establish
2. Increased finances as there are many members. They can also borrow from banks since they have better security
3. Management is easy as work is shared
4. No chances of being overworked and there is room for holidays
5. Experience can be brought in and specialization can be practiced
6. The accounts of this business unit are private

Disadvantages of a Partnership

1. Unlimited liability; members are liable for the acts of others
2. Delays in decision making because all partners must be consulted
3. Uncertainty of the partnership in case one member dies or retires
4. Limited finances because membership is restricted to 20

Similarities between Sole Proprietorship and Partnership

1. Unlimited liabilities
2. Limited life

3. Profit maximization
4. Few legal formalities
5. Limited source of capital
6. Do not declare source of capital

Limited Companies/Joint Stock Company

A company is an association of individuals organized for the purpose of carrying out business with a view to making profit. They undertake large scale operations. Limited companies may be divided into two types:

1. *The Private Limited Company* – this form develops from a partnership or family business that needs to expand beyond the resources of the partners
2. *The Public Limited Company* – this form embraces the very largest manufacturing units in the private sector. It must have at least seven members, but there is no maximum limit

Features of Limited Companies

1. *Legal personality* – A joint stock company is an association of persons created by law
2. *Shares* – The capital of the company is divided into shares and each share is transferrable
3. *Perpetual succession* – A company exists until it is liquidated. The death of one shareholder does not

affect the existence of the company

4. **Board of Directors** – the company is managed by a Board of Directors who are elected by the shareholders

5. **Limited liability** – Each shareholder is liable only up to the amount of capital contributed

6. Members cannot bind a company by their acts; they act in accordance with the regulation of the company

Advantages of Limited Companies

1. Limited liability
2. Continuity of business
3. Specialization
4. Share of loss

Disadvantages of Limited Companies

1. Expensive to set up
2. Delay in decision making
3. Non-participation of shareholders in management
4. Difficult to control the company as management becomes more complex with the growth of the company
5. Double taxation as the shareholders and the company are taxed
6. Limited companies have to pay interest every year irrespective of performance

Public Corporation

A public corporation is a form of enterprise where the government decides to place production in the hands of the state. A public corporation is run and managed by the state for the benefit of the public. They help in providing public goods and their aim is not to make profits. They are run by a Board of Directors appointed by the Government.

Co-operative Societies

A co-operative society is a business unit formed with the purpose of benefitting members.

Types of Co-operative Societies

1. *Consumer co-operative societies* – These are formed for the purpose of trading. Individuals come together and buy goods cheaply, which they sell to members
2. *Producer co-operative societies* – These deal with the marketing of agricultural products and some of them are involved in production
3. *Transport co-operative societies* – These deal with transportation
4. *Savings and credit societies* – These are co-operatives that mobilize savings and provide credit to members

SHORT RUN AND LONG RUN ANALYSIS

Short run is a time period which is not long enough for the firm to adjust all factors of production so as to be variable. In the short run one of the factors of production is fixed.

Fixed Inputs are the inputs which don't change with changes in output. Their value remains the same whether output increases, decreases or there is no production, e.g. rent, salary for watchman, etc.

Variable Inputs are inputs which change with changes in output. As the output increases, variable inputs will also increase, e.g. raw materials, labour, etc.

Long Run is a period which is long enough for the firm to adjust all factors of production so as to be variable.

In the long run all factors of production are variable.

Measures of Productivity

Productivity means output per unit input, e.g. productivity of labour is output per worker.

There are three measures of productivity:

1. *Total product (TP).*

This is the maximum amount of output that can be produced from a given set of inputs. It refers to the final goods and services produced from a given set of inputs

2. *Average product (AP).*

This is the total output per unit input, e.g. average product of labour is the output per worker.

If 40 workers produce 600 units of output, calculate the average product of labour

$$AP = \frac{\text{Total output}}{\text{Labour units}} = \frac{Q}{L}$$

$$^{600}/_{40}$$

$$= 15 \text{ Units}$$

Interpretation: Every worker gives 15 units of output

3. *Marginal product (MP)*

This is the change in total output due to an additional 1 unit of input, e.g.

$$MP_L = \frac{\text{Change in output.}}{\text{Change in labour}} = \frac{\text{change in Q}}{\text{change in L}}$$

When the number of workers increased from 30 to 36, the total output decreased from 720 to 600 units. Calculate the marginal productivity of labour

$$\frac{\text{New output} - \text{old output}}{\text{New }_L - \text{Old }_L}$$

$$= \quad 600 - 720$$

$$\overline{}$$

$$36 - 30$$

$$= -^{120}/_6 = -20$$

PRODUCTION IN THE SHORT RUN

The Law of Variable Proportions or the Law of Diminishing Returns

In production all factors are not fixed. Usually land is fixed and all the other factors are variable. In the short run the firm can increase the amount of output by increasing the amount of variable inputs, while other factors of production are fixed. Initially, as the amount of variable inputs increase, total output also increases, but the increase will not be indefinite. As the amount of inputs continues to increase, total output increases at a lower rate or starts decreasing. This is referred to as the *law of diminishing returns or Stages of Production.*

The law can be explained by the use of an illustration and a graph as follows:

Illustration

No. of workers	Total Product (TP)	Average Product (AP)	Marginal Product (MP)
1	8	8	8
2	20	10	12
3	36	12	16
4	48	12	12
5	55	11	7
6	60	10	5
7	60	8.6	0
8	56	7	-4

Graph

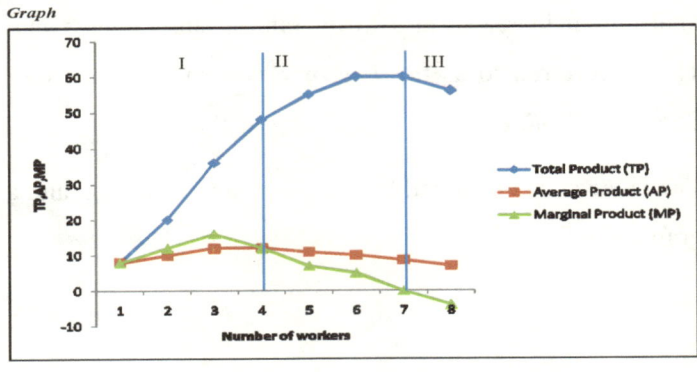

122

Stages of Production

Stage I- Stage of increasing returns

Marginal product is increasing. Due to increasing marginal product, total product and average product also increase. At this stage the cost of production decreases as output increases, because firms enjoy economies of scale or increasing returns to scale

Stage II- Stage of decreasing returns

At this stage total product increases and reaches maximum. Both marginal products and average products decrease but are still positive. It is logical to continue producing at this stage.

Stage III- Stage of negative returns

The total product and average product decreases while marginal product is negative. It is illogical to produce at this stage.

Assumptions of the Law of Diminishing Returns

1. Technology does not change
2. The units used can be divided into smaller units
3. Short run situation
4. Only one factor is variable and others fixed; one factor must be fixed

5. All units of the variable factor are homogeneous

6. Factors are divisible

Returns to Scale

This shows how output changes when inputs change. There are four stages of returns to scale

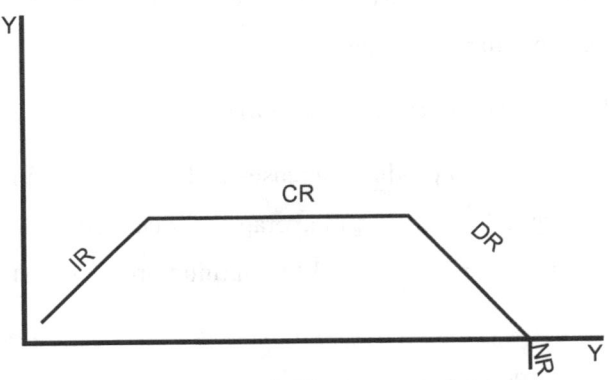

1. Increasing returns to scale

This occurs when inputs are doubled, and output increases but more than double

2. Constant returns to scale

This occurs when inputs are doubled, and output also doubles

3. Decreasing returns to scale

This occurs when inputs are doubled, and output increases, but less than double

4. Negative returns to scale

This occurs when inputs are doubled, and output is negative

Economies of Scale

Economies of scale are the advantages a firm enjoys due to large-scale production.

The ATC decreases as production increases.

There are 2 types of economies of scale:

1. Internal Economies of Scale
2. External Economies of Scale

Internal economies of scale

These are the advantages a firm enjoys due to large-scale production.

Types/sources of internal economies of scale

1. Financial economies

Large-scale firms with a lot of capital and assets can secure bank loans easily for expansion purposes. They can attract many investors who contribute a lot of capital for business expansion purposes

2. Managerial economies

Large firms with a lot of capital can employ experienced and qualified workers. This leads to better business decisions and quality services, which satisfy customers and make a lot of profit compared to small firms

3. Marketing economies

Large firms with a lot of capital can advertise their products, leading to increased sales and profits compared to small firms

4.Risk-bearing economies

Large firms with a lot of capital can invest in many projects and sell their products in many markets. In case one project fails, profits can be obtained from other projects or markets

5.Research economies

Large firms can carry out research on how to improve product quality, or new methods of production, and hence they are able to satisfy customers

6.Purchasing economies

Large firms with a lot of capital buy raw materials in large quantities and are able to get discounts accruing from bulk buying. These reduce costs and help them to make huge profits

7.Technical economies

Large firms with a lot of capital can use advanced technology and heavy machinery. Specialisation is possible; production is faster and efficient, leading to increased output at a lower cost and hence higher profits

External economies

These are the advantages a firm enjoys due to the growth of

other firms within the industry or the existence of other firms in that area.

Sources of external economies of scale

1. Ready market for the product
2. Availability of raw materials
3. Security
4. Availability of social facilities such as: banks, schools, hospitals, etc.
5. Good infrastructures: e.g. roads, electricity, etc.
6. Availability of skilled labour

Diseconomies of Scale

These are disadvantages a firm faces due to large scale production

1. The average cost increases as production increases
2. Decision making and implementation is slow because it must pass through many processes
3. There are chances of over-production, leading to wastage of goods and thus losses
4. There is poor personal contact between owners and customers
5. There is a poor relationship between employees and employers
6. There is competition over factors of production, leading to shortage and increased price

7. There are high running costs arising from advertising, wages, etc.

ISOQUANT

The term 'isoquant' is derived from Latin words 'iso' meaning equal and 'quant' meaning amount. The isoquant is also known as the equal product curve, or production indifference curve. An isoquant curve is a locus of points representing the various combinations of two inputs, labour and capital, yielding the same output. The fact that different input combinations can produce the same output is based on the assumption that capital and labour can be substituted for one another, but at a diminishing rate.

Assumptions

1. That a producer uses only two inputs; labour (L) and capital (K) to produce a commodity (X)

2. That labour and capital can be substituted for one another at a diminishing rate

3. That technology does not change and that it is given for the period under reference

4. That the production function of the firm is continuous; i.e., labour and capital are perfectly divisible and substitutable

Properties of Isoquants

Like indifference curves, isoquants have the following properties:

1. ***Isoquants have a negative slope:*** Isoquants have a negative slope in the economic region or in the relevant range. Economic region is the region on the isoquant plane in which substitution between inputs is technically possible. It is also known as the profit maximizing region. The negative slope of the isoquant implies that if one of the inputs is reduced the other must be increased, so that the output remains the same.

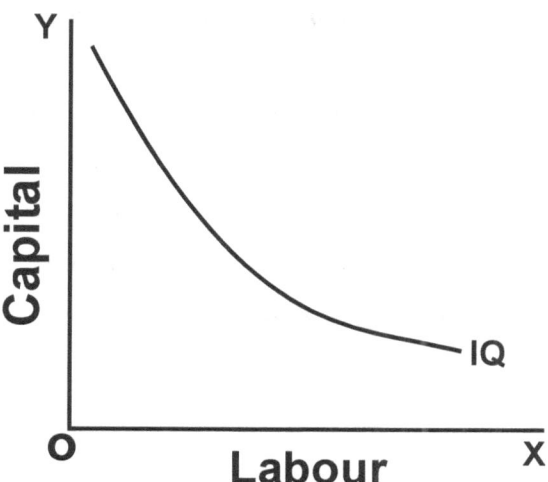

2. **Isoquants are convex to the origin:** Convexity of the isoquants signifies the substitution of one factor for the other and the diminishing rate of technical substitution.

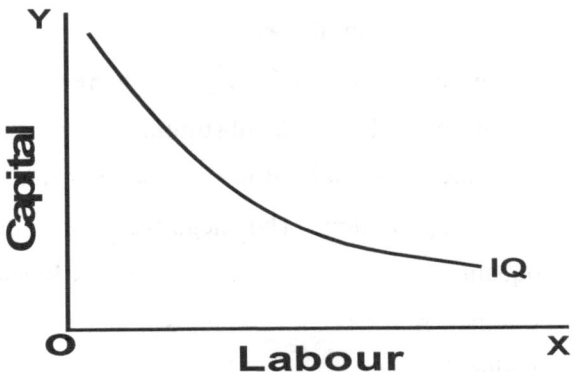

3. **Isoquants cannot intersect or be tangent to each other:** The intersection or tangency of two isoquants implies that a certain quantity of a commodity can be produced with a smaller input combination, as well as with a larger input combination. This is not consistent with the theory of production, so long as the marginal productivity of an input is greater than zero.

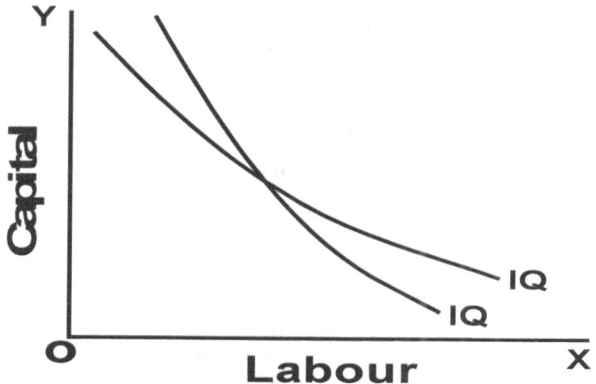

PRODUCTION POSSIBILITIES

Production possibilities refer to the alternative combinations of goods and services that a society is capable of producing with its given resources and state of technology. For example, a country can produce two commodities, tea and coffee, alternatively, by making use of its resources and technology. The combinations of tea and coffee that a country chooses to produce on the PPF depend on the demand for tea and coffee. This can be explained by the use of a table or a curve. The curve is known as the production possibility frontier (PPF).

Alternative Production Possibilities

Alternatives	Tea (Thousand Tons)	Coffee (thousand Tons)
A	100	0
B	80	15
C	70	35
D	60	55
E	45	70
F	20	85
Z	0	95

Production Possibility Frontier

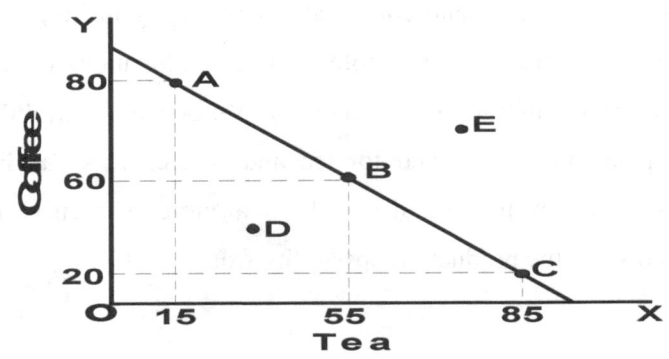

Any point below the PPF means there is underutilization of resources. Any point above the PPF is not attainable due to lack of resources.

THEORY OF COSTS

Costs are expenses incurred in the production process.

There are various types of costs:

1. Opportunity cost
This is the value of the best left/foregone alternative

2. Fixed costs (FC)
These are the costs which do not change with changes in output. Their value remains the same whether output increases, decreases or there is no production; e.g. rent, watchman's salary, etc.

3. Variable costs (VC)
These are costs which change with changes in output. As output increases, variable costs also increase and vice versa, e.g. raw materials, salaries of casuals, etc.

4. Total costs (TC)
This is the sum of fixed costs and variable costs. TC = FC + VC

5. Average fixed costs (AFC)
This is the total fixed costs per unit output produced

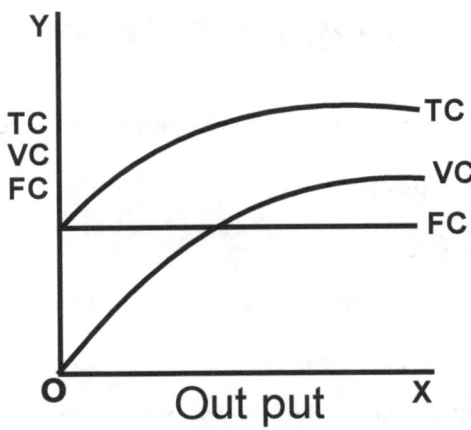

AFC decreases as output increases, hence it is downward sloping

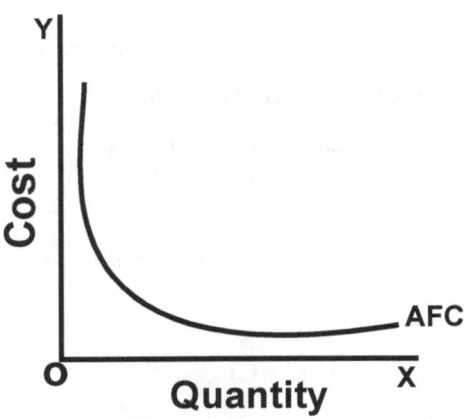

6. Average variable costs (AVC)

This is the total variable costs per unit output produced

AVC = Variable cost
──────────────
Total output

$= {}^{VC}/_{Q}$

7. Average total costs (ATC or AC)

This is the total cost per unit output produced

ATC = ${}^{TC}/_{Q}$ = Total cost
──────────────
Total output

8. Marginal costs (MC)

This is the change in total cost due to a change in output. It shows how costs change due to an additional production of 1 unit of output

MC= Change in total cost= ${}^{\Delta TC}/_{\Delta Q}$

Change in total cost

Example

The total costs increase from Kshs. 200 to Kshs. 320 when the total output is increased from 700 to 800 units. Calculate the marginal costs

M.C =Change in total cost= ${}^{\Delta TC}/_{\Delta Q}$
──────────────
Change in total cost

$$= \frac{320 - 200}{800 - 700}$$

$$= {}^{120}/_{100}$$

$$= 1.2$$

Short run AFC, AVC and ATC curves

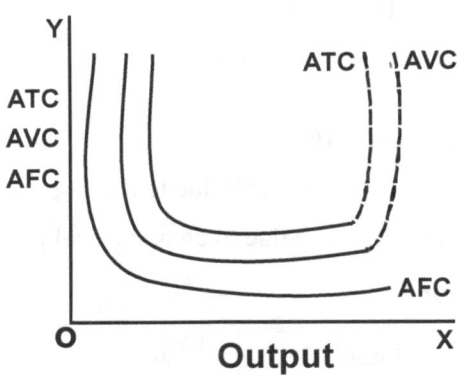

An AFC curve is downward sloping. This indicates that AFC falls as output increases. Initially, AVC decreases as output increases due to the law of *diminishing returns*, as the firm faces decreasing or negative returns to scale. Because of this, the AVC and the ATC curves are U-shaped. When the AVC decreases as output increases, the MC also falls and, later, as the AVC increases as output increases, the MC will also start rising.

Revenue

Revenue is the total sum of money received by the firm from the sale of a given level of output. There are three concepts of revenue:

1. Total Revenue (TR)

This is the total sum of money received by the firm from the sale of a given level of output

Total Revenue = Price per unit x Total output sold

$TR = P \, x \, Q$

2. Average Revenue (AR)

This is the total revenue received per unit sold

Avenue Revenue = Total Revenue _____

 Total Output sold

$AR = TR \, /Q$

Since $TR = PQ$ Then $AR = {}^{PQ}/_Q = P$

3. Marginal Revenue (MR)

This is the change in TR due to a change in total output sold. It shows the additional revenue received from the sale of an additional unit of output

Marginal Revenue (MR) = Change in total Revenue

                                Change in output

$M.R = \Delta \, TR/\Delta Q$

In a perfect competitive market where there are many buyers and sellers, the market price is determined by the market forces of demand and supply:

Price	Output	Total Revenue (TR)	Average Revenue (AR)	Marginal Revenue (MR)
7	1	7	7	7
7	2	14	7	7
7	3	21	7	7
7	4	28	7	7
7	5	35	7	7
7	6	42	7	7
7	7	49	7	7

In a perfect market P=AR=MR

Profit Maximisation

One of the objectives of the firm is to maximize profits. Profit is the difference between Total Revenues and Total Costs:

Profit = Total Revenue – Total Costs

$P = TR - TC$

There are various concepts of profits:

1. Normal profits

This is the minimum level of profits required to maintain the existing firms in their present production, but yet not enough to attract new firms in the market.

Normal profits are made when Total Revenue is equal to Total Cost:

Normal Profits = Total Revenue - Total Cost = 0

$= TR - TC = 0$

TR = TC (breakeven point)

2. Abnormal Profits

These are the profits over and above the normal profits

TR>TC or TC<TR

TR – TC = Abnormal profits

3. Losses

These are the losses made when revenue is less than costs or costs are more than revenue

TC>TR or TR<TC or TR – TC = losses

Rule of Profit Maximization

The firm maximizes profits when it produces the level of output at a point where MR = MC, as long as the MC curve cuts the MR curve from below. At this point where MR = MC, it means that TR = TC, meaning that TR – TC = 0 (normal profits). At this point the firm is at equilibrium or at rest; it cannot increase production since it is not gaining and cannot decrease production because there is no loss. If MR>MC, the firm is not at equilibrium, because it will want to produce more so as to make more profits. If MC>MR, the firm is not at equilibrium, because it may want to reduce production so as to minimize losses.

CHAPTER FIVE

MARKET STRUCTURE

MEANING

Market structure refers to factors such as the number of firms in the industry, the size of the firm, the ease with which firms enter or leave the market etc., which determine the behaviour and performance of the firm selling products in the market.

Depending on the market structure, we have various types of markets:

    a) Perfect competitive market

    b) Monopoly

    c) Monopolistic competition (Duopoly)

    d) Oligopoly

    e) Monopsony

PERFECT COMPETITION

This is a market structure having many buyers and sellers selling homogeneous/identical products. This type of market is common in the agricultural sector, e.g. eggs, tomatoes, maize, beef, etc.

Features of a Perfect Competitive Market

1. There are many buyers and sellers – No single seller influences the market, e.g. price
2. Free entry and exit – There are no limitations such as licenses to entry and exit
3. The products are homogeneous
4. The aim of the firm is to make profits
5. Both buyers and sellers have perfect knowledge about the market, i.e. they know the market price and quality
6. Both buyers and sellers are price takers because both buy at market price, which is determined by demand and supply
7. The demand curve facing each firm is perfectly elastic; i.e. a small increase in price by one firm causes a big decrease in quantity demanded
8. Buying and selling any amount at the market is possible because there is no Government control
9. There is perfect mobility of factors of production; i.e. factors can be switched from loss making areas to areas where they can make a profit

Market Demand Curve and Individual Firm Demand Curve

In this market the market price is determined by the market forces of demand and supply. The market price is determined at a point where the demand and supply curves meet. There is no single seller who can influence the market price and each firm must sell the product at the market price. Therefore the market price and the market demand curve is the individual market price and individual demand curve, represented by a horizontal line.

Market Demand Curve

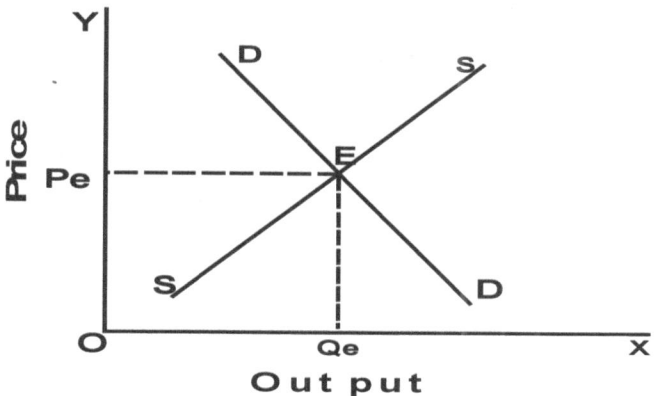

Individual Demand Curve

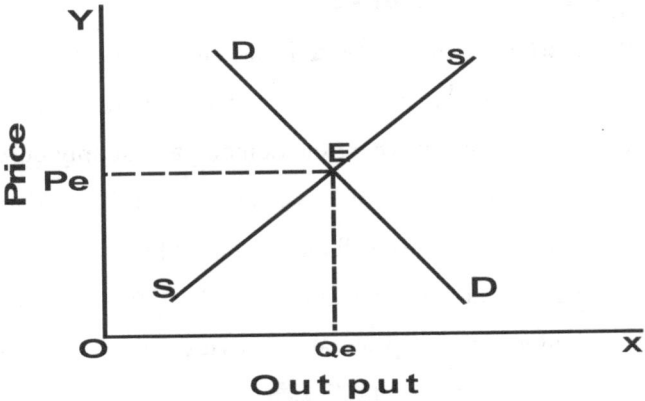

Equilibrium of a Perfect Competitive Market

The firm is at equilibrium when it produces the level of output that maximizes profit. This occurs at a point where MR = MC, as long as the MC curve cuts MR curve from below. It is possible for the firm to make losses, abnormal profits or normal profits in the short run, even when MR = MC but this depends on the position of the AC curve.

Making losses in the short run

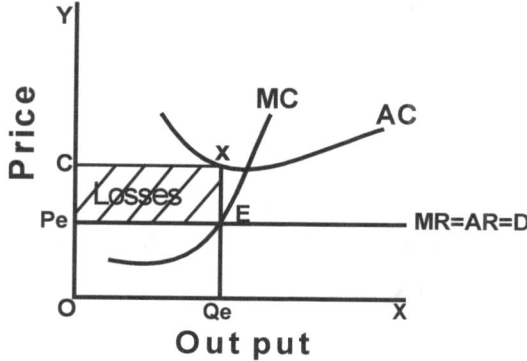

The firm is at equilibrium when it produces the level of output at the point where MR = MC at E and produces output Qe

TR = PeQe

TC = QeC

Hence TC>TR, meaning TR – TC = Losses, are shown by the shaded area PeCXE

Abnormal profits

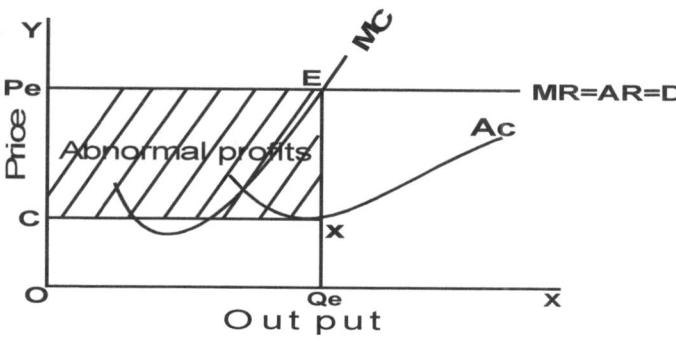

The firm is at equilibrium when it produces the level of output at the point where MR = MC at E and produces output Qe

TR = PeQe

TC = QeC

Here TR>TC, meaning TR –TC = Profits, as shown by the shaded area CPeEX

Normal profits

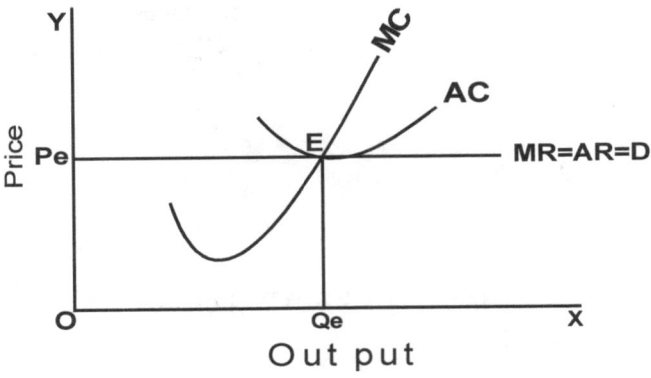

The firm is at equilibrium when it produces the level of output at the point where MR = MC at E and produces output Qe

At point E, AC = AR, TR = TC, meaning TR – TC = 0, hence normal profits.

Advantages of perfect competitive market

1. Consumers have a wide choice because there are many sellers
2. Production of quality products arising out of competition
3. There is no consumer exploitation as consumers pay the market price
4. There are no monopolies to exploit the consumers
5. There is no wasteful competition, e.g. advertising costs

Disadvantages of a perfect competitive market

1. Consumers lack a wide variety of choice because products are homogeneous
2. Firms make only normal profits in the long run
3. Stiff competition may lead to the collapse of weak firms
4. Closing down of some firms will lead to unemployment
5. This may lead to unequal distribution of income in the economy
6. Since firms aim at maximizing profits, they do not account for externalities, e.g. pollution
7. There is no room to provide public goods for the benefit of the general public

Why firms in a perfect competitive market make normal profits in the long run

Firms in a perfect competitive market make only normal profits in the long run. When firms make excess profits, new entrants are attracted to the market. Production and supply increases and prices start to decrease. Firms now start making losses. Losses make some firms quit the market and supply decreases, thus making prices go up. This happens because entry and exit is free. Firms are at equilibrium when they make normal profits at a point where TR = TC, meaning TR − TC = 0 (normal profits). When normal profits are made, there are no incentives for new firms to enter the market and existing firms to quit the market.

MONOPOLY

This is a market having many buyers and one seller selling a product which has no close substitute and there are barriers to entry which prevent other firms from entering the market. Since there is only one seller, then there is no difference between the seller and the market.

Characteristics of Monopoly

1. There are many buyers
2. There is one seller
3. The product has no close substitute
4. There are barriers to entry, e.g. licenses, patent rights,

etc.

5. There is no competition among the sellers

6. The seller is the price maker and the buyer is the price taker

7. The demand curve facing the firm is downward sloping, because the seller must lower the price to sell more

8. The aim of the producer is to maximize profits

Sources of Monopoly

1. *Government License* – The Government may give permission to only one firm to produce a certain product, which prevents other firms entering the market

2. *Patent Rights* – The Government may give permission to only one firm to be producing and supplying a certain product for a specific number of years

3. *Starting Capital* – When the initial capital required to start the business is so huge that only one firm can afford it, then such a firm becomes a monopoly

4. *Existence of Goodwill* – When customers have identified a certain firm as the best in the market because of the products it offers, new firms entering the market do not get customers and are forced to quit

5. *Restrictive Practices* – Firms may decide to merge,

take over others or form a cartel and operate as one

6. *Ownership of Strategic Raw Materials or Technology* – When important raw materials and technology needed to produce a certain product are owned by one firm, then such a firm becomes a monopolist

7. *Natural Factors* – Climatic or geographical features may favour the production of a certain product in one area and not the other areas

8. *Limiting Price* – Established firms may fix very low prices, pushing their competitors out of business

Price Discrimination

This is where the seller charges different prices for the same product to different consumers in different markets, e.g. a medical doctor charging a different fee for the same treatment among the poor and the rich.

Types of price discrimination

1. *Time:* The same product is charged at different prices according to time, e.g. peak and off peak, day and night, etc.

2. *Geographic:* The same product is charged at different prices according to the street, location, area, town, country, etc.

3. *Brand:* The same product is branded differently and

sold at different prices

4. *Use:* Some products are sold at different prices according to use, e.g. electricity charges differ between domestic and industrial use

Conditions for price discrimination

1. The seller should be able to divide the market into sub markets and each sub market should have different elasticity of demand

2. The supply should be in the hands of a monopolist who controls the market

3. The seller should know that there are consumers who are willing and able to pay more than the market price

4. The cost of separating the market should be relatively cheap

5. There should be no chance of reselling; i.e. a product bought in market 1 cannot be sold in market 2

6. Ignorance and laziness: For price discrimination to take place, there should be some consumers who are ignorant that the same product is cheaper in another market, or those who are aware are too lazy to go and buy in a cheaper market

Price and Output Determination

A monopolist is a price maker because he determines the market price but does not determine the quantity buyers should buy. The demand curve facing monopolists is downward sloping because to sell more he has to lower prices. Due to this, both the MR and AR curves are downward sloping but most originate from the same point.

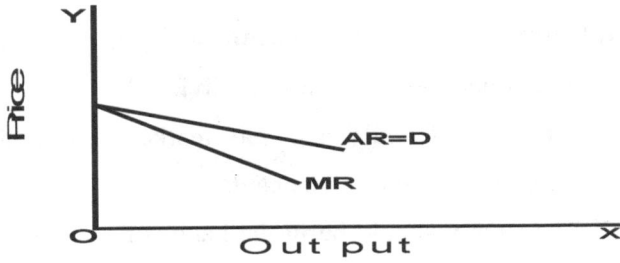

Equilibrium of a monopolist firm

The firm is at equilibrium when it produces the level of output that maximizes profits. This occurs at a point where MR = MC. It is possible for the monopolist firm to make losses, abnormal profits or normal profits even when MR = MC. This is true both in the short run and long run, depending on the position of the AC curve, but the long run losses do not last for long.

Losses

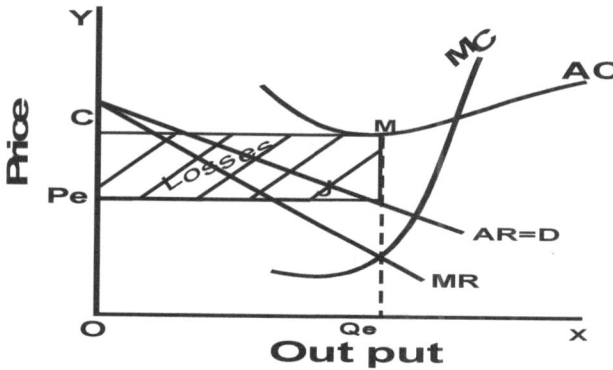

The firm is at equilibrium when it produces the level of output where MR = MC at point E and produces output Qe.

TR = PeQe.

TC = QeC.

Here TC>TR, meaning TR − TC = losses, as shown by the shaded area PeCKX

Abnormal Profits

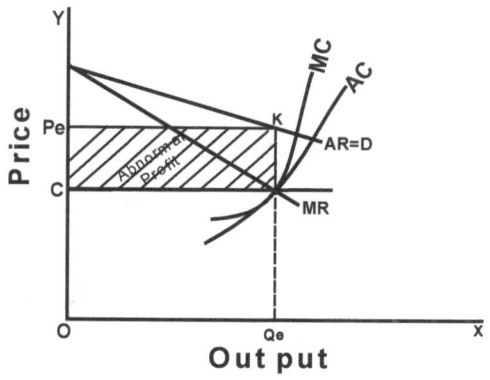

The firm is at equilibrium when it produces the level of output that maximizes profits at the point where MR = MC at point E and produces Qe

TR = PeQe

TC = QeC

Here TR>TC, meaning TR – TC = profits, as shown by the shaded area PeCGM

Normal Profits

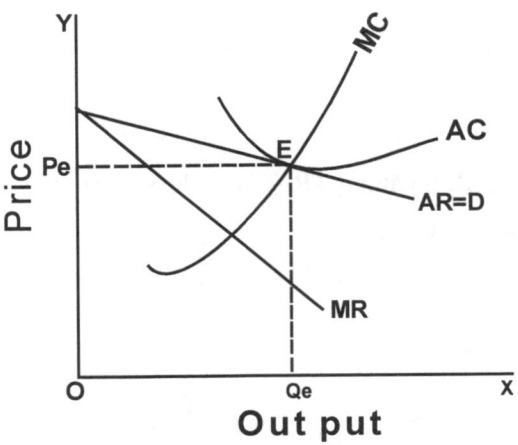

Out put

The firm is at equilibrium when it produces a level of output that maximizes profits at the point where MR = MC at point E1 and it produces output Qe. At point M, AR = AC, meaning TR = PeQe; TC = PeQe; Hence TR = TC and TR – TC = 0 (normal profits).

Advantages of Monopoly

1. It is a way of protecting local industries, e.g. through patents

2. Monopolies operate on a large scale. They enjoy economies of scale and this may benefit consumers by getting goods at a lower price

3. Monopolies earn abnormal profits in both the short run and long run

4. High profits earned by monopolies lead to increased Government revenue through taxes

5. There is no wasteful competition, e.g. advertising costs

6. There is no wastage of resource, e.g. through duplication and over-exploitation of resources

7. Monopolies can use price discrimination to provide essential services to the poor

8. Monopolies can use excess profits for research and development, leading to improved quality of products

Disadvantages of monopoly

1. Due to lack of competition low quality products are produced

2. Abnormal profits may lead to unequal distribution of income

3. Consumers are exploited through over-charging

4. Consumers lack freedom of choice and are therefore forced to accept what the monopoly offers
5. Sometimes the monopolists restrict the amount offered in the market, leading to artificial shortage, which in turn leads to inflation
6. Sometimes they do not develop new products; they buy technology and hide it

Control of Monopoly

1. The Government should give licenses to many firms wishing to enter into the market dominated by monopolies
2. The Government should pass laws that make the existence of monopolies illegal
3. The Government should buy and own monopoly businesses
4. The Government should fix prices of essential products
5. The Government should heavily tax the profits of monopolies

MONOPOLISTIC COMPETITION

This is a market having many buyers and sellers selling differentiated products. Product differentiation is where one firm attempts to distinguish its products from the products of its competitor, e.g. by use of colour, shape, brand, advertising, model, being friendly, etc. Examples of monopolistic competition are the car industry, cosmetics, clothes, etc.

Features of Monopolistic Competition

1) There are many buyers and sellers
2) Products sold are differentiated
3) Entry and exit is free
4) The aim of the firm is to make profits
5) There is non-price competition, i.e. firms do not reduce prices to attract customers but use other methods such as giving gifts
6) Firms face a downward sloping demand curve
7) Normal profits in the long run

Price and Output Determination in Monopolistic Competition

Due to product differentiation each firm can exercise influence over the market price. Though products are competing substitutes, some consumers display loyalty to certain products and view the others as poor substitutes. To increase the demand for the product, firms must reduce the product price; hence the demand curve is downward sloping.

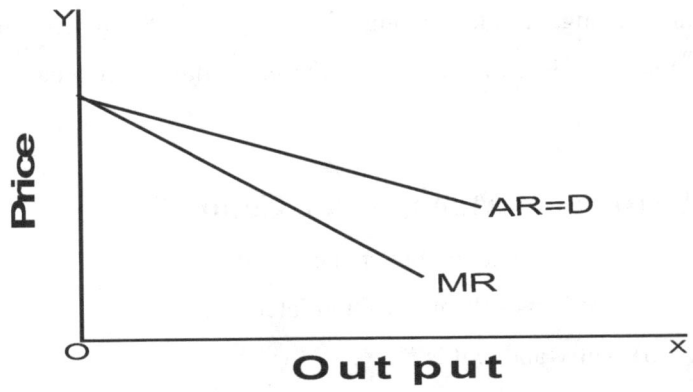

Equilibrium of the Firm

The firm is at equilibrium when it produces the level of output that maximizes profits. This occurs at a point where MR = MC. It is possible for the firm to make normal profits, losses and abnormal profits in the short run, even when MR = MC, but this depends on the position of AC curve.

Losses in the Short Run

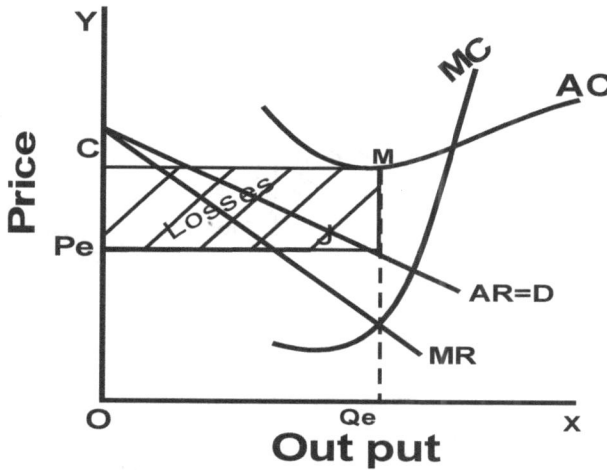

The firm is at equilibrium when it produces the level of output that maximizes profits at a point where MR = MC at K and produces Qe.

TR = PeQe   TC = CQe

Here TC>TR, meaning TR – TC = losses, shown by the area PeCMJ

Abnormal Profits

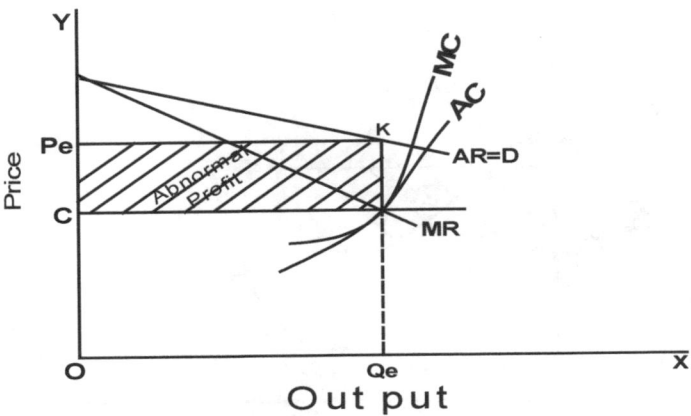

The firm is at equilibrium when it produces the level of output that maximizes profits at a point where MR = MC at P and produces Qe.

TR = PeQe   TC = QeM

Here TR>TC, meaning TR – TC = Profits, as shown by the shaded area MPeKX

Normal Profits

Normal profits

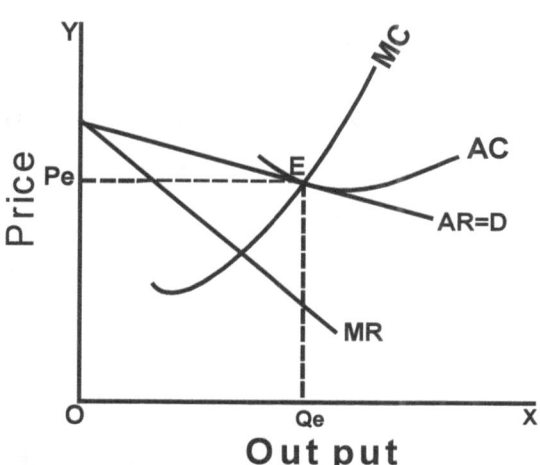

The firm is at equilibrium when it produces the level of output that maximizes profits at point E, where MR = MC and produces Qe.

At point G, AR = AC, meaning TR = TC, given by

TR = PeQe

TC = PeQe

Hence TR − TC = 0 (normal profits)

In the long run the monopolistic firm makes normal profits. Abnormal profits made in the short run attract many firms to the market, since entry is free, and firms now start making losses. Losses force some firms to quit the market, such that firms are at equilibrium in the long run when they make normal profits. When normal profits are made there are no incentives for new firms to enter the market and existing firms to quit the market.

Advantages of monopolistic competitive market

1. Consumers have choice because there is a variety of differentiated goods
2. Consumers have choice because there are many sellers to choose from
3. Competition among producers leads to production of high-quality goods
4. Prices are stable due to non-price competition and this helps consumers to plan ahead on their spending
5. Since firms earn normal profits in the long run, it leads to equal distribution of income in the economy

Disadvantages of monopolistic competitive market

1. There is wasteful competition, e.g. on advertising
2. There is no technological progress because firms imitate each other's innovations, e.g. persuasive advertising, eye-catching packaging etc.
3. There is wastage of resources due to duplication of products

It is worthwhile to note the difference between monopoly and monopolistic competition. Monopoly is a market with a single seller and many buyers and has a unique product while monopolistic competition is a market with many buyers and sellers with differentiated products.

OLIGOPOLY

This is a market structure having many buyers and few sellers selling homogeneous or differentiated products. Firms are relatively large and each firm dominates the market. Examples of this system are the newspaper industry, gas stations, mobile phones, the banking industry, the dairy industry, etc.

Features of Oligopoly

1. Many buyers
2. Few sellers
3. There are barriers to entry, e.g. license, advertising, etc.
4. There is mutual interdependence among sellers when it comes to making decisions on price and output; i.e. sellers consult each other before changing the price
5. Prices remain stable/rigid for a long time due to interdependence
6. Products sold are homogeneous or differentiated

7. There is non-price competition; i.e. the sellers do not reduce the price to attract customers but use other methods
8. In this market it is difficult for each firm to determine the demand curve
9. Sometimes firms collude

Price and Output Determination

In an oligopolistic market it is difficult to be certain about the effect of price change on the demand for the product. If one firm changes the price, the quantity demanded for the product depends on the reactions of rival firms; e.g. if one firm reduces its price the other firms may react by reducing their prices, retain their original prices or increase their prices. A firm must take into consideration the reaction of other firms when making decisions on price and output.

Collusion

This is a way of avoiding uncertainties in the market. It involves firms coming together and entering into an agreement aimed at maximizing joint profits. Firms fix the common price and agree the amount to be supplied by each firm into the market.

Forms of collusion

Cartel

A cartel is formed when such an agreement is open and formal. A cartel acts as a monopoly (single seller) e.g. OPEC. In many countries cartels are illegal

Tactical collusion

When such an agreement is made by word of mouth and secretly

Price leadership

One firm sets the price and the other firms follow it

Non-collusion oligopoly

Here firms do not collude and do not coordinate their activities. In this case, firms expect reactions from other firms and firms have never learnt from past mistakes. The model used to explain non-collusive oligopoly is called the *kinked demand curve*. It is also called the *Sweezy model*

The Kinked Demand Curve (the Sweezy Model)

The kinked demand curve hypothesis is developed by Paul M Sweezy (Paul M Sweezy, Demand Under Conditions of Oligopoly," Journal of Political Economy, Vol XLVIII, August 1939, reprinted in American Economic Association, Readings in Price Theory). Kinked demand curve hypothesis is used for explaining the price and output determination under oligopolywith product differentiation.

Assumptions:

The kinked demand curve hypothesis of price rigidity is based on the following assumptions:

1. There are few firms in the oligopolistic industry.

2. The product produced by one firm is a close substitute for the other firms.

3. The product is of the same quality. There is no product differentiation.

4. There are no advertising expenditures.

5. There is an established or prevailing market price for the product at which all the sellers are satisfied.

6. Each seller's attitude depends on the attitude of his rivals.

7. Any attempt on the part of a seller to push up his sales by reducing the price of his product will be counteracted by the other sellers who will follow his move.

8. If he raises the price, others will not follow him. Rather they will stick to the prevailing price and cater to the customers, leaving the price-raising seller.

9. The marginal cost curve passes through the dotted portion of the marginal revenue curve so that changes in marginal cost do not affect output and price.

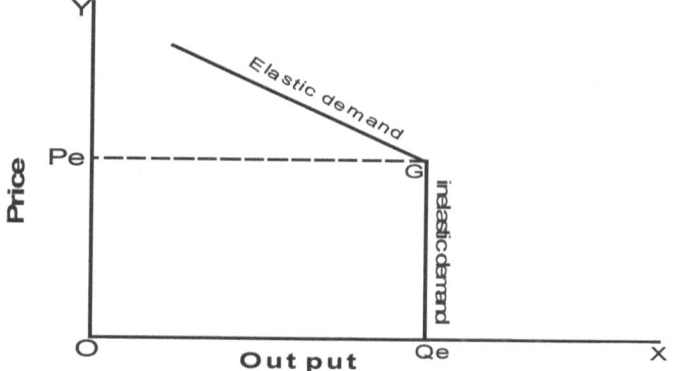

If one firm increases the price, rival firms will not increase their prices and hence demand is elastic with regard to price increase. This is because any increase of price above Pe will lead to a big loss in market share. If one firm reduces the price, other firms are forced to reduce theirs to avoid losing customers. Demand is inelastic with regard to price reduction. Following the two arguments, firms are faced with a kink where the two demand curves meet. The effect is that it creates a situation of prices remaining stable for a relatively long time. Firms do not benefit by increasing or reducing the price.

This tends to explain why prices in oligopolistic markets remain stable for a relatively long time. Firms face a downward sloping demand curve with a kink at the current price; i.e. there are two demand curves in one with a kink where they meet.

167

Advantages of oligopoly

1. Firms operate on a large scale and enjoy economies of scale
2. Prices are stable and this helps consumers to plan their spending ahead
3. Consumers have choice because there is a variety of differentiated products
4. Firms make a lot of profit which they can use on research and development to improve quality

Disadvantages of oligopoly

1. Firms collude and exploit customers by overcharging
2. Collusion leads to lack of competition and products produced are of poor quality
3. There is wastage of resources because firms duplicate the products of other firms

DUOPOLY

Duopoly is a type of oligopoly where only two producers exist in a market. Two firms own all or nearly all of the market for a given type of product or service, e.g. Kenya Breweries and Keroche Industries; and previously Safaricon and Kencel. There are two main models of duopoly and these are:

1. Cournot Duopoly

Here the two firms assume each other's output and take this as a fixed amount. They produce their products according to this benchmark

2. Bertrand Duopoly

The two firms assume the other will not change its prices in response to its price cuts. When both firms use this logic they reach a *Nash Equilibrium.* A Nash Equilibrium is a solution concept of a game involving two or more players. Each player is assumed to know the other's strategies

Features of Duopoly

1. There is price control resulting in price stability
2. There are only two firms in the market/industry
3. There are very strong barriers to entry
4. They use non-price competition

Advantages of Duopoly

1. There is close competition, ensuring quality products
2. The firms interact with each other a lot
3. Low prices, as firms react to each other's price cuts
4. Simple markets

Disadvantages of Duopoly

1. In some cases prices will not drop even after reaching a Nash Equilibrium

2. The market can go stale due to lack of new products
3. Two huge firms in the market make it difficult for small firms to gain recognition
4. New firms die out before they are able to generate competition

MONOPSONY

A *monopsony* is a *market* similar to a monopoly except that a large buyer, not a seller, controls a large proportion of the *market* and drives prices down.

1. A monopsony occurs when a firm has market power in employing factors of production (e.g. labour).
2. A monopsony means there is one buyer and many sellers.
3. It often refers to a monopsony employer – who has market power in hiring workers.
4. This is a similar concept to monopoly where there is one seller and many buyers.

Monopsony in Labour Markets

An example of a monopsony occurs when there is one major employer and many workers seeking to gain employment.

If there is only one main employer of labour, then they have market power in setting wages and choosing how many workers to employ.

Examples of monopsony in labour markets

- Coal mine owner in town where coal mining is the primary source of employment.
- Government in employment of civil servants, nurses, police

Diagram of monopsony

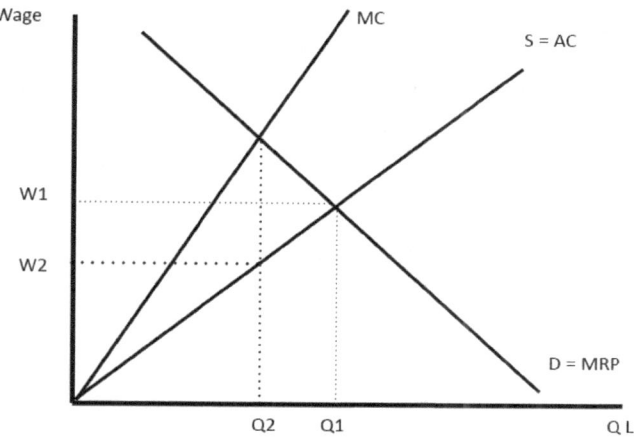

- In a competitive labour market, the equilibrium will be where D=S at Q1, W1.
- However, a monopsony can pay lower wages (W2) and employ fewer workers (Q2)

Profit Maximisation for a Monopsony

- The marginal cost of employing one more worker will be higher than the average cost because to employ one extra worker the firm has to increase the wages of all workers.

- To maximise the level of profit, the firm employs Q2 of workers where the marginal cost of labour equals the marginal revenue product MRP = D

- In a competitive labour market, the firm would be a wage taker. If they tried to pay only W2, workers would go to other firms willing to pay a higher wage.

Minimum wage in a monopsony

In a monopsony, a minimum wage can increase wages without causing unemployment.

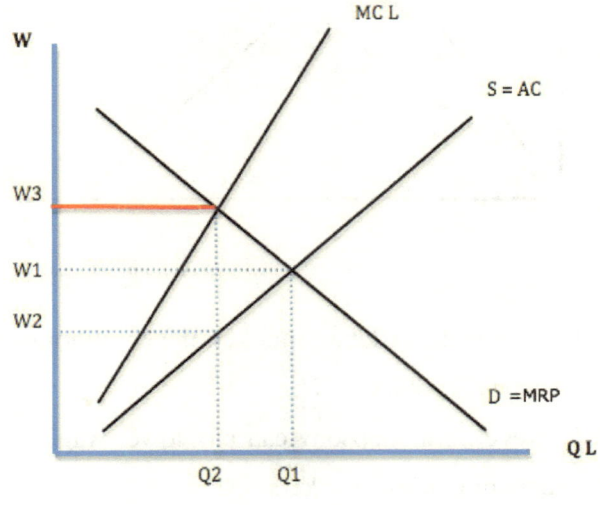

www.economicshelp.org

- A monopsony pays a wage of W2 and employs Q2.
- If a minimum wage was placed equal to W1, it would increase employment to Q1.

- A minimum wage of W3 would keep employment at Q2.

Monopsony in the real world

Even if a firm is not a pure monopsony, it may have a degree of monopsony power, due to geographical and occupational immobilities, which make it difficult for workers to switch jobs and find alternative employment.

For example, there are several employers who might employ supermarket checkout workers. However, in practice, it is difficult for workers to switch jobs to take advantage of slightly higher wages in other supermarkets. There is a lack of information and barriers to moving jobs. Therefore, although there are several buyers of labour, in practice the big supermarkets have a degree of monopsony power in employing workers

Problems of monopsony in labour markets

- Monopsony can lead to lower wages for workers. This increases inequality in society.
- Workers are paid less than their marginal revenue product.
- Firms with monopsony power often have a degree of monopoly selling power. This enables them to make high profits at the expense of consumers and workers.

- Firms with monopsony power may also care less about working conditions because workers don't have many alternatives to the main firm.

Monopsony in product markets

In several industries, there is one buyer and several sellers.

- Supermarkets have monopsony power in buying food from farmers. If farmers don't sell to the big supermarkets, there are few alternatives. This has led to farmer protests about the price of milk.
- Amazon.com is one of the biggest purchases of books. If publishers don't sell to Amazon at a discounted price, they will miss out on selling to the biggest distributor of books.

CHAPTER SIX

NATIONAL INCOME

MEANING

National income refers to the total money value of final goods and services produced in the country during one year, measured at current prices.

Abbreviations

Y – National Income

Py – Personal Income, which is the income received per individual

T – Taxes. These are compulsory contributions imposed by the Government on people from which no direct benefits are obtained

Yd – Disposable income. This is the income left after taxation

C – Consumption. This is the money spent on goods and services

S – Savings. This is the money left after consumption. $S = Yd - C$

G – Government Expenditure. This is the money spent by the Government to provide public goods and services

X – Exports. These are goods and services we sell to other countries

M – Imports. These are goods and services we buy from other countries

I – Investment. This is the money spent on capital goods; e.g. machinery, industry, buildings, etc.

GDP – Gross Domestic Product. This is the total money value of final goods and services produced within a country during one year

NDP – Net Domestic Product. NDP = GDP – Depreciation

GNP – Gross National Product. This is the total money value of final goods and services produced within a country during one year plus incomes earned by our nationals abroad

NNP – Net National Product. NNP = GNP – Depreciation

Methods of Measuring National Income

1. Output Approach
2. Income Approach
3. Expenditure Approach

Output Approach

The output produced by all sectors in the economy is added together; e.g. Agriculture = 40b, Mining = 30b, Fishing = 20b, Tourism = 100b etc. National Income = 190b

The output approach reveals the performance of each sector.

The output approach has various shortcomings:

1. Double counting – some output is counted twice if final goods are not distinguished from the immediate goods; e.g. mangoes and mango juice
2. Records on production are available only from large firms and not from small ones
3. Illegal production is not counted because it does not exist in the open market; e.g. production of cocaine, prostitution

Income Approach

Here all incomes earned in form of wages, salaries, interests, dividends, etc. are added together, excluding any income earned which is not accompanied by current production; e.g. pension, donations, prizes, grants, etc.

Expenditure Approach

All forms of spending on final goods and services are added together. Spending on intermediate goods is excluded to avoid the problem of double counting.

The national income identity is that:

Income Approach (Y), Output Approach (Q) and

Expenditure Approach (E) should give us the same value.

General Problems in Measuring National Income

1. *Double counting* – some output is counted twice if

final goods are not distinguished from intermediate goods and this gives us the wrong figure of national income

2. *Lack of statistical data* on income and production. Due to high illiteracy levels many people don't keep records on income and production, especially in poor countries

3. Calculation of *depreciation* is a problem because there is no accepted standard measure of depreciation

4. It is difficult to know where to place *incomes earned by foreign firms*; i.e. whether to place them where they are operating or in the country of origin

5. *Some activities defy measurement* – e.g. housewife services, own shaving, half-completed house, etc.

6. *Illegal activities* are not counted because they not exist in the open market; e.g. hard drugs, gambling, prostitution, etc.

7. *Lack of reliable statistical data* on incomes and production because most people give false information about their income and production

8. *Existence of non-monetary sector* is a problem because people carry out trading activities through barter trade and hence there are no records

9. It is difficult to measure *non-marketed output* – e.g. meals eaten at home and meals sold in hotels

10. *Lack of occupational specialization* – Most people in

poor countries engage in many activities as a source of earning income and it is difficult to get their incomes from all the sources

11. *Information on production* is available from large firms and not from small ones

Determinants of the Level of National Income

1. *Availability of factors of production in terms of quantity and quality* – a country with enough quality factors of production is likely to produce more output and will have high levels of national income

2. *Political situation in the country* – wars discourage investment, production decreases and the country will have low levels of national income

3. *Availability of natural resources, e.g. minerals, oil, etc.* – a country with enough natural resources, e.g. oil, will have high levels of national income

4. *Level of technology* – with advanced technology, more output is produced with the same amount of resources and the national income will increase

5. *Working population* – this is determined by population size and structure, attitude of people towards work, availability of jobs, etc. In a country where many people are working the national income is high

Importance of National Income Statistics

1. It measures the overall performance of the economy, e.g. per capita income, and thus helps to show the living standards of the people in a country

2. It helps to compare the living standards of people between countries

3. It helps to show the contribution of each sector to GDP

4. It also helps the Government in planning and policy making because it indicates the trends (changes) in employment, inflation, etc.

5. Business communities may use the figures to know the market trends so as to invest appropriately; e.g. to know which sector is growing and which sector is declining

Per Capita Income and the Standard of Living Among Countries

Per Capita income is the average income which passes through the hands of every individual in the country during one year.

$$\text{Per Capita Income} = \frac{\text{Total National Income}}{\text{Total Population}}$$

In many cases it is measured in US$.

Per capita income is a measure of the standard of living of people such that a country with a higher per capita income has a higher standard of living and is thus a richer country. Standard of living means the quality of life of people in a country determined by the kind of food eaten, shelter, education, sanitation, friends, etc.

Why it is not appropriate to use Per Capita Income in Determining Living Standards

It is not always the case that a country with a high per capita income has a population enjoying high living standards for the following reasons:

1. Unequal distribution of income – increased national income may be in the hands of a few people while the masses are poor

2. Increased national income may be achieved through poor working conditions; e.g. child labour, forced labour, etc.

3. Inaccurate estimate in total national income – Some countries underestimate and others overestimate the total national income and this gives the wrong figure of per capita income

4. Inaccurate estimate of total population also gives the wrong figure of per capita income

5. Increased national income may be achieved at the expense of leisure, thus people are being overworked.

In such a country people have low living standards

6. Per capita income does not take into account negative externalities, e.g. pollution, which may affect many people negatively in the country

7. Increased national income may lead to increased public immorality – People may use the income on heavy drinking, gambling, hard drugs, prostitution etc.

8. Existence of differences in tastes and preferences towards cheap and expensive things – in one country people may prefer cheap things and in another they may prefer expensive things

9. Existence of differences in price and currencies between countries means that the value of national income will differ from country to country

Circular Flow of Income

This describes how income circulates in the economy. Circular flow of income shows income moving from firms to households and from households to firms.

Circular flow of income in a two-sector economy

A two-sector economy is a *closed* economy. There is no international trade and there is no Government.

It only has two agents:

1. Firms
2. Households

Assumptions of a two–sector economy

1. Households own all factors of production, e.g. land, labour, etc. which they provide to firms
2. Households receive factor payments from firms in return, e.g. rent, wages, etc.
3. Firms produce goods and services for households
4. Households spend all the income received from the firms to buy goods and services produced by the firms
5. There is no saving for investment purposes

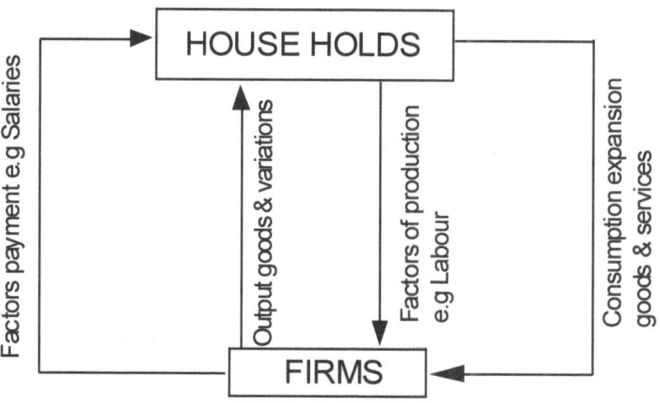

Households provide all factors of production and receive factor payments in return.

Households use the income received from the firms to buy goods and services produced by the firms and the process is continuous, hence it is called *circular flow of income.*

Circular Flow of Income in a Four-sector Economy

A four-sector economy is also called *an open economy*

It is open to the rest of the world through international trade.

The economy has four agents:

1. Firms
2. Households
3. International trade – meaning there are exports and imports
4. Government – meaning there are taxes and Government activities

This type of economy deals with *leakages* and *injections.*

Leakages

This consists of all factors which reduce the circular flow of incomes between the households and firms and these factors are:

1. Savings (S) by households or firms reduce the circular flow of income between households and firms
2. Taxes (T) by the Government reduce incomes among

households and firms

3. Imports (M) – income spent on imported goods means that overseas firms are paid

Injections

These are the factors which increase the circular flow of income between households and firms and these factors are:

1. Exports (X) – these bring money from other countries

2. Government expenditure (G) – Government expenditure on projects means that workers are paid money

3. Investment (I) – investment increases production and income among firms and households

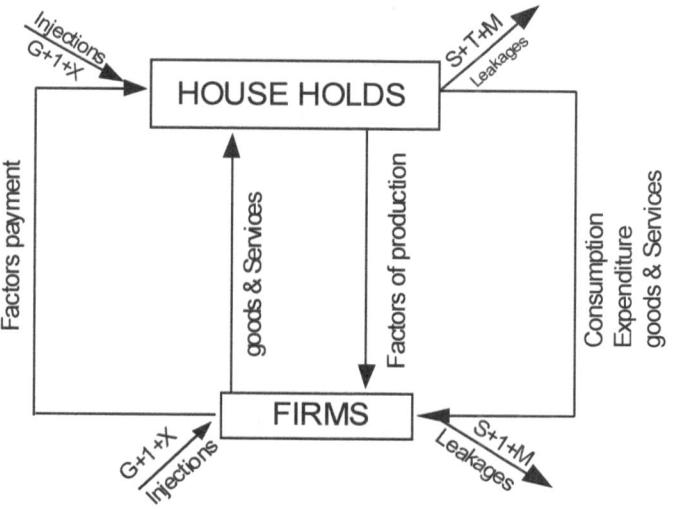

Trade Cycle/Business Cycle

A trade cycle is a tendency of income and employment to fluctuate over time in a sequence of ups and downs. The fluctuations can be observed by examining annual changes in the income of a country over a number of years.

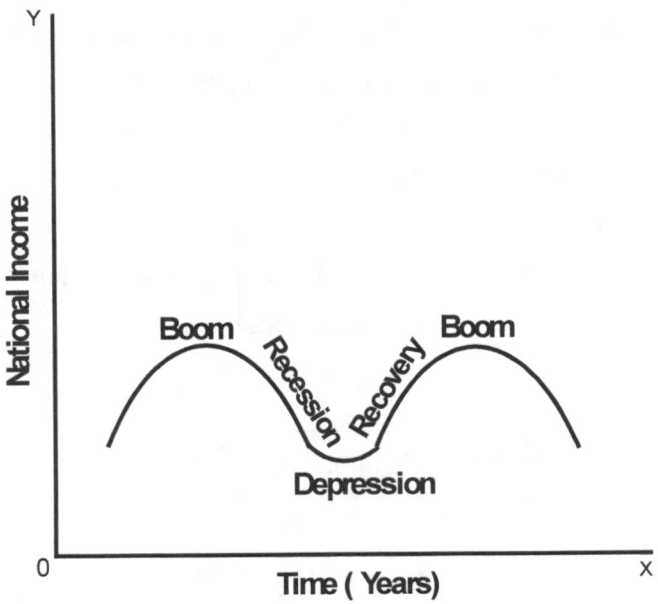

Trade Cycle Phases

Boom

This phase is characterized by the following:

1. High national income
2. Increased demand for goods and services
3. High prices for goods and services

4. Low levels of unemployment

5. Increased investment

6. Firms operate at full capacity

7. Decreased poverty levels

Recession

1. National income starts decreasing

2. Demand for goods and services decreases

3. Prices start decreasing

4. Investment decreases

5. The country starts becoming poor

6. Employment levels start to decrease

Slump/Depression

1. National income is low

2. Prices are low

3. There are high levels of unemployment

4. Investment decreases because investors have lost confidence in the country

5. The poverty level is very high

6. Decreased demand for goods and services

7. Firms operate at under capacity

Recovery

After some time, the country starts recovering.

1. National income starts to increase

2. Demand for goods and services increases

3. Prices for goods and services increase
4. Investment increases
5. Employment level starts to increase
6. Poverty levels decrease

Characteristics of a Trade Cycle

1. The phases occur periodically
2. The phases occur in a sequence of ups and downs
3. Prices and output change in each phase
4. Slump/depression occurs faster than recovery

Consumption

Consumption is utilization. Consumption expenditure is the income spent on goods and services. In a two-sector economy where there is no Government or international trade, income received by individuals is consumed and the remainder saved.

$Y = C + S$

Y – Income

C – Consumption

S – Savings

The consumption function is given as:

$C = b_0 + b_1 Y$

b_0 is autonomous consumption

Autonomous consumption does not depend on income, and thus does not change with changes in income. It must be there whether one has income or not.

Sources of Autonomous Consumption

1. Stealing
2. Begging
3. Borrowing
4. Conning
5. Savings

b_1 is induced consumption, also called *marginal propensity to consume* (MPC). This is the consumption which depends on income. MPC shows how consumption changes when income changes by 1 unit. It is the slope of the consumption function.

Average Propensity to Consume

This is the ratio of consumption to income. It shows the average income out of the total income used on consumption.

$APC = C/Y$

E.g. if $Y = 10,000$ and $C = 8,000$

$APC = C/Y; 8,000/10,000 = 0.8$

Interpretation: This means that 80% of the total income is used on consumption.

Savings

This is any income left after consumption

Since $Y = C + S$ then $S = Y - C$

Given $C = b0 + b1Y$ then $S = Y - b0 - b1Y$

$\qquad = Y - b1Y - b0$

$S = Y(1 - b1) - b0$

$Ds/dy = 1 - b1$; this is called Marginal Propensity to Save.

MPS shows how savings change when income changes by one (1) unit. b0 is called autonomous savings; savings which do not depend on income hence do not change with changes in income.

Average Propensity to Save (APS)

This is the ratio of savings to total income.

$APS = S/Y$

Always $MPC + MPS = 1$

If MPC is equal to 1 it means that all the income is spent on consumption and such a person is very poor because there are no savings for investment purposes.

Reasons for Saving

1. For precautionary purposes, i.e. for a rainy day, meaning to meet unexpected events such as sickness,

visitors, etc.

2. To buy assets, e.g. cars, land, etc.
3. For investment purposes, e.g. paying school fees
4. Saving from habit

Since people save in order to invest, then S = Investment.

If Y = C + S then Y = C + I

Investment

This is the additional capital stock in the country, e.g. buying machines, building industries, etc. We have two types of investments:

1. *Financial investment–* This is where individuals invest in financial assets; e.g. shares, bonds, etc. In economics, this is not real investment because it involves the transfer of ownership of papers from one person to another. In this case no new jobs are created, no more production, etc.

2. *Real investment* – This is investment in real assets; e.g. buying machines, building industries, etc.

Factors Determining Investment

1. Interest Rate – Most investments are funded by loans from banks. As the interest rate increases, loans become more expensive and investment decreases
2. Political situation in the country. Wars discourage

investment

3. Economic conditions, e.g. inflation or deflation, discourage investment

4. The level of confidence among investors about the future

Multiplier

The *multiplier* refers to the ratio of change in national income to initial change in autonomous expenditure that brought it about; e.g. investment, Government expenditure, exports, etc. The multiplier measures the effect on total national income of a unit change in one of the components of aggregate demand; e.g. I, G, X, etc.

The *multiplier effect* refers to the increase in final income arising from any new injection of spending. The size of the *multiplier* depends upon household's marginal decisions to spend, called the marginal propensity to consume (mpc), or to save, called the marginal propensity to save (mps).

$K = \underline{1}$

1- MPC

Accelerator Principle

This refers to the theory that the level of aggregate investment depends on the expected change in output. According to the accelerator principle, the increase in demand for goods will lead to an increase in investment. This is because increase in demand for goods will force producers to increase investments so as to produce more goods to meet the increased demand. The accelerator theory is an economic postulation whereby companies' investments increase when either demand or income increases. ... The accelerator theory posits that companies typically choose to increase production, thereby increasing profits.

Assumptions

1. **No Excess Capacity in Consumer Goods Industries** - If there is already excess capacity in the consumer goods sector, a rise in demand for consumer goods will not lead to any induced investment or acceleration effects, because the increased demand may be met from the existing capital and machinery without producing additional capital goods.

2. **Surplus Capacity in Investment Goods Industries** - On the other hand the operation of the principle depends upon the presumption that there is surplus capacity in the investment goods industries. If it were not so, i.e., no excess capacity existed in machine-making industries, an increase in the derived demand

for machines would not induce an increased supply of machines.

3. **Nature of Demand** - The increase in the demand for consumption goods must be more or less permanent in nature to have acceleration effects. A purely temporary increase in the demand for consumer goods will not lead to any addition in the capital goods.

4. **Capital-Output Ratios** - The principle of acceleration is based on the assumption that there is a constant ratio of the output of consumer goods and capital equipment needed for their production i.e., there is constant capital output ratio. In reality this ratio is not necessarily constant.

5. **Availability of Resources** - The working of the investment accelerator principle is further restricted by the availability of resources and the ability of the machine-making industry to produce more-machines. In order that the increased demand for capital goods be followed by an increase in production there must be enough unemployed resources available for employment in the capital goods industries i.e., these industries should be able to expand.

6. **Elastic Credit Supply** - The elastic supply of credit is another factor which helps in the smooth working

of the investment acceleration principle. Whenever there is induced investment as a result of induced consumption, enough credit should be forthcoming for investment in investment-goods industries.

7. **Fluidity** - Operation of the acceleration is also based on the assumption that the investment-goods industry is in fluid condition. It assumes that ".... finished goods are turned out as fast as wanted and materials and means of production are instantly supplied as fast as the process of finishing requires them." There is no loss of production in time.

Criticism of the Accelerator Theory

The principle of acceleration has come in for a good deal of criticism in recent years. For example, it has been pointed out by Kaldor that we cannot assume a constant value of the accelerator throughout the trade cycle, that is, it is not true that an increase in output or income by an amount must always give rise to a multiple increase in investment.

This is because, if already, some machines are lying idle, we shall try to use them before rushing in for new equipment. Also, if expectation of entrepreneurs is that the rise in demand brought about by increase in income or output is only a temporary one, they will try to meet it by overworking the existing machinery rather than installing a new plant. Thus, in the theory of accelerator it has been assumed that there is no excess capacity existing in consumer goods industries.

In other words, it has been assumed that no machines are lying idle and no extra shift working is possible. If there had been excess capacity and extra shift working was possible, the supply of goods could be increased with the existing equipment and the accelerator would not come into play.

Further, in the acceleration principle it has also been assumed that in the capital goods industries, there exists surplus productive capacity. If there is no excess capacity in the machine-making industries, increased demand for machines caused by the requirement for additional output would not lead to increase in the supply of machines.

In the absence of supply of machines, investment cannot increase in the short run. It is thus assumed in the accelerator theory that the machine-making industry is capable of increasing its output for the time being at least. The supply can be increased by reducing stocks of finished machines, by working extra shifts, and so on. But stocks cannot be reduced below zero and working double shifts or adoption of other experiments is found to be expensive. Only when the demand has increased permanently, will the entrepreneurs find it worthwhile to increase investment in machine-making industries.

The size of the accelerator does not remain constant over time. Its value will be affected by the businessmen's calculation regarding the profitability of installing new plants to make more machines on the basis of their probable working life. It is also assumed that the demand for machines will remain stable in future, although the increase in demand has suddenly cropped up.

However, in spite of the above limitations of acceleration principle, it points out an important force which causes economic fluctuations in the economy. Economists like Samuelson, Hicks and Dusenberry have shown how accelerator combined with multiplier provides an adequate and satisfactory theory of business cycles that occur in free market economies.

CHAPTER SEVEN

UNEMPLOYMENT

MEANING

Employment refers to a situation where a person is engaged in any income-earning activity; this can be in the public sector, private sector or self-employment. A person is considered *unemployed* if he or she is above 18 years, is willing and able to work, and has been looking for a job but cannot find one.

Problems Associated with Unemployment

1. Low output in the economy
2. Poverty level in the country increases
3. Per capita income decreases
4. High dependence ratio
5. Low Government revenues from taxes
6. Increased income inequality
7. Slow economic growth and development
8. Increase in crimes such as theft
9. Increase in social problems such as prostitution, divorce, drug abuse, etc.

Types of Unemployment

1. Frictional Unemployment
2. Structural Unemployment
3. Demand deficiency/cyclical unemployment
4. Seasonal Unemployment
5. Disguised Unemployment

Frictional Unemployment

This arises when a qualified person cannot fill the existing vacancies in the labour market due to lack of information about the labour market. In this case the employers and job seekers do not match.

Frictional unemployment occurs when:

1. A person quits a job in search of another one
2. New workers enter the labour market but have no information on where to get jobs
3. Lack of mobility of labour due to high social costs, e.g. losing family ties

Structural Unemployment

This occurs due to technological changes in the economy; e.g. the introduction of computers will affect many secretaries or those people without IT skills. Also, new technology like DVDs will affect the tape-recorder industry.

Demand Deficiency Unemployment

This is caused by a decrease in demand for goods and services resulting from low purchasing power. This leads to the closing down of some industries, hence loss of jobs. Demand deficiency is caused by:

1. Reduced Government expenditure, meaning people have less money to spend
2. Taxes on products making them expensive and hence reduced demand
3. Dumping of cheap goods from other countries, e.g. second-hand clothes, leads to closing down of local industries
4. Increased tax on personal income reduces demand
5. Reduction in money supply

Seasonal Unemployment

This is unemployment caused by climatic changes in the economy, especially in the agricultural and tourism sectors. We have droughts and off seasons.

Disguised Unemployment

This is also known as *hidden unemployment*. This occurs when there is not sufficient work to effectively occupy the workers. In this case, even if some workers are withdrawn, work will not be affected.

General causes of unemployment

1. High population growth rate leading to more labour supply than demand

2. Dumping of cheap goods leading to closure of local industries

3. High taxes on personal income leading to reduced demand for goods

4. Use of inappropriate technology in production (mainly capital intensive) increases unemployment

5. Job discrimination based on gender, tribe, age, etc.

6. Lack of information about job opportunities

7. Lack of training and education

8. Corruption and nepotism

9. Rural – Urban migration causing urban unemployment

10. Low savings, hence low investment

11. Poor education system that does not give adequate skills

Policy Actions to Control/Curb Unemployment

Fiscal Policy Measures

This involves the use of taxes, Government expenditure, public borrowing and public debt management to reduce unemployment in the economy. To alleviate unemployment the following measures can be taken:

1. The Government can increase its expenditure, e.g. in public projects like roads, to create jobs
2. Increase tax on cheap imports to protect local industries
3. Reduce personal income tax so as to enhance demand for goods. This will in turn lead to higher production and employment
4. Reduce taxes on products so that their demand increases, which will be followed by increased employment
5. Reduce public borrowing so as to encourage private sector investment
6. Increase public debt repayment so as to make more money available to the public

Monetary Policy Measures

This involves controlling the quantity of money available and cost of money (interest rate) in the economy.

1. The Government, through the Central Bank, can advise commercial banks to reduce the interest rate on loans. This makes loans cheaper for investment
2. Increase money supply through open market operations (OMO) by buying Government securities
3. Reduce the cash reserve ratio so that banks can lend money for investment
4. Reduce the compulsory deposit amount so that

commercial banks can have money to lend

5. Avoid selective credit control so as to lend money to all

Other Measures

1. Population control through family planning
2. Improved education system that can absorb graduates
3. Use of appropriate technology, e.g. labour-intensive techniques
4. Total ban on cheap imports to protect local industries
5. Control rural-urban migration by developing rural areas
6. Adopt 'one man one job' policy
7. Wage cuts, though difficult, can reduce production costs. This will in turn reduce prices, and increase demand for goods; production will increase and create more employment
8. On-the-job training to reduce structural unemployment
9. Control inflation and deflation
10. Setting up of employment offices to provide information
11. Supporting the informal sector (juakali) for self-employment

Philips Curve

The **Phillips curve** given by A.W. **Phillips** shows that there exist an inverse relationship between the rate of unemployment and the rate of increase in nominal wages. Philips said that there was a close link between the level of unemployment and the rate of wage increase. He discovered that there was a stable relationship between the rate of wage increase and the level of unemployment. It may also be considered a relationship between inflation and unemployment, because when there is inflation wages invariably go up under trade union pressure. A lower rate of unemployment is associated with higher wage rate or inflation, and vice versa.

The Philips curve shows this relationship:

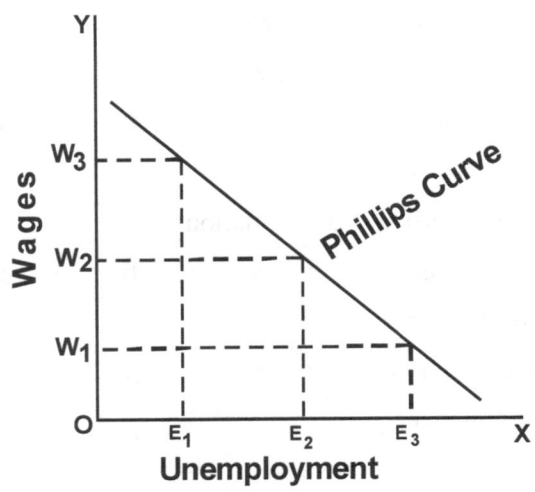

CHAPTER EIGHT

INTERNATIONAL TRADE

MEANING

International Trade is trade between countries. It involves export and import trade. *Export trade* is the selling of goods and services to other countries. *Import trade* is the buying of goods and services from other countries.

Advantages/Benefits of International Trade

1. It enables a country to obtain goods and services that it cannot produce
2. It creates employment to people involved in trade
3. It acts as a source of Government revenue
4. It enables a country to get a variety of goods produced in other countries
5. It promotes good relationships between countries
6. Competition among countries leads to production of quality goods
7. It promotes specialization among countries
8. During natural calamities/disasters a country can get supplies of essential goods from other countries
9. It promotes modern industries, as machinery and technology can be transferred from rich countries to poor ones

10. It creates international understanding between countries as traders move from one country to another
11. It earns foreign exchange for the country through exports
12. It enables a country to dispose of surplus products which could have been wasted

Disadvantages

1. Harmful goods may be imported into the country, e.g. contaminated milk, expired goods, etc.
2. Some imported goods have negative effects on the culture of a country, e.g. pornographic literature, drugs, etc.
3. It makes a country poor if imports exceed exports
4. It may make a country tolerate bad practices from another country due to over dependency on that country's imports
5. Overspecialization and over dependence on one product may create problems when the product is exhausted, or due to fluctuations in world market prices
6. During war the supply of essential goods, e.g. oil, is not guaranteed

Free Trade Versus Protection

Free Trade

Free trade means there are no barriers, e.g. quotas, tariffs, etc. In this case countries are free to trade with each other.

Advantages of Free Trade

1. Promotes peace among countries
2. Consumers get goods at lower prices because there is no payment of taxes
3. Enables consumers to have a variety of goods produced in other countries
4. Promotes specialization among countries
5. Competition among countries leads to production of high-quality products
6. Importation of raw materials becomes easy
7. It promotes the movement of factors of production among countries and this reduces unemployment

Disadvantages of Free Trade

1. Some countries dump cheap goods in other countries
2. Some countries import more than they export and this leads to an unfavourable balance of payments (BOP) in the affected countries
3. The dumping of cheap goods may lead to the closing down of industries
4. It causes unemployment

5. Governments see free trade as a loss of revenue that could have been received from taxes

Protection

This means there are trade barriers, such as tariffs, quotas, etc. When a country finds that it is losing more than gaining from international trade, it may decide to protect her industries against unfair competition from foreign firms.

Methods of Protection

1. *Total Ban* – This is where the Government says no to the importation of certain products
2. *Fixing Import Quotas* – This is fixing the maximum amount of imports into the country
3. *Applying Import Licence* – This is meant to limit the amount of imports in the country as acquiring them is cumbersome
4. *Foreign Exchange Control* – The Government, through the Central Bank, may sell foreign exchange to some importers on some essential goods and deny those importing luxuries
5. *Government Control Over International Trade* – In this case the importing and exporting will be done by the Government
6. *Boycott* – The locals can boycott the consumption of foreign goods if they are produced locally

7. *Devaluation* – This is a deliberate action by the Government, through the Central Bank, to lower the value of the local currency. This makes imports expensive and exports cheap

8. *Embargos* – These are trade sanctions aimed at weakening a political enemy

9. *Import Duties* – Import duties make imported goods expensive

10. *Red Tape* – This involves increasing processes and documents needed in importing goods to discourage some importers

11. *Voluntary Agreements* – These can be made between countries on the amount of imports and exports

12. *Incentives* – These can be given to producers of exports, e.g. free loans, to make them competitive in the world market

Advantages for Protection

1. To stop dumping of cheap goods
2. To stop importation of harmful goods
3. To protect local infant industries
4. To create a market for local goods
5. To create employment
6. It acts as a source of Government revenue from taxes, import duties, etc.
7. For political reasons, e.g. to weaken political enemies

Disadvantages of Protection

1. May lead to poor relationships between countries
2. It may lead to under-utilization of resources as it is not based on specialization and division of labour
3. Consumers will lack a variety of goods produced in other countries
4. Due to lack of competition from other countries poor-quality goods will be produced
5. May lead to monopolies, which may exploit consumers by exploiting/overcharging
6. May lead to a decrease in trade as the level of imports and exports decreases
7. May lead to wastage of goods due to less exporting

The Theory of Absolute Advantage

In economics, the principle of absolute advantage refers to the ability of a party (an individual, or firm, or country) to produce a greater quantity of a good, product, or service than competitors, using the same amount of resources. The theory states that a country should specialize in the production of goods that it can produce at a lower cost than any other country. The country can consume what it requires and export the surplus, using the money earned from exports to buy goods and services which she cannot produce from a country that produces them at a lower cost.

	Coffee	Computer
Kenya	2	200
Britain	50	5

Assume that two countries, Kenya and Britain, produce two goods, for example computers and coffee. It takes Kenya 200 days to produce a computer and five days to produce a bag of coffee. It takes Britain two days to produce a computer and 50 days to produce a bag of coffee. The theory of absolute advantage requires that Kenya should specialize in the production of coffee and Britain in computers.

The Theory of Comparative Advantage

Comparative advantage refers to the ability of a party to produce a particular good or service at a lower opportunity cost than another. Even if one country has an absolute advantage in producing all goods, different countries could still have different comparative advantages. The theory states that a country should specialize in producing a commodity which it can produce at a lower opportunity cost than its trading partners. A country will export goods for which it has a relative lower production cost and import a product for which it has relatively high production cost.

Illustration

	Coffee	Cocoa
Kenya	10	25
Ghana	8	4

Assume that two countries, Ghana and Kenya, produce two goods, namely coffee and cocoa. It takes Ghana 8 days to produce a bag of coffee and 2 days to produce a bag of cocoa. It takes Kenya 10 days to produce a bag of coffee and 25 days to produce a bag of cocoa. Ghana has the advantage of producing both goods cheaply. Specialization in international trade (the theory of comparative advantage) requires that a country specializes in the production of one commodity. Hence Ghana will choose to produce the commodity with the least opportunity cost, which is cocoa.

Assumptions of the theories

1. There are trade restrictions
2. A country is not able to be self-reliant
3. It assumes there are no transport costs
4. It assumes countries have similar resources
5. Countries have similar tastes and preferences
6. It assumes prices are the same
7. Both countries share the same currency

Balance Of Payments

This is a summary statement showing economic transactions between citizens of a country and the rest of the world. It shows the total value of imports and exports of a country for one year.

It consists of:

a) *Visible trade* – This is the trade in goods whose value is recorded at the ports, e.g. cars, tea, coffee, computers, etc.

b) *Invisible trade* – This is the trade in services whose value is not recorded at the ports, e.g. tourism

A balance of payment has two accounts:

1. *Current account* – This account records the total value of imports and exports of a country during one year

(This includes both visible and invisible trade)

2. *Capital account* – This shows the flow of funds between countries, e.g. loans, grants, interest, etc.

When the total value of imports is greater than the total value of exports, the country experiences an unfavourable balance of payments/disequilibrium BOP/BOP deficit. Most poor countries experience unfavourable BOP.

Causes of unfavourable BOP

1. When the level of imports keeps on increasing while the level of exports keeps on decreasing

2. Natural calamities such as drought, meaning that there is no production

3. Political instability, particularly wars, affect production negatively, hence there is no production for exports

4. Most poor countries produce similar goods, leading to excess supply or no demand in the international markets

5. Most poor countries produce primary goods, e.g. tea, which fetch low prices compared to manufactured goods, e.g. machines, which they import

6. Restrictions by trading partners which protect their industries reduce the level of export

7. Overvaluation of the local currency makes imports cheaper and discourages exports

8. Rich and industrious countries protect their industries and this reduces exports from poor countries

9. High population growth, which means that whatever is produced is consumed at home, hence there is no surplus to export

Strategies to reduce unfavourable BOP

1. *Total ban* – The Government can ban the importation of certain products, e.g. second-hand clothes

2. *Import quotas* – The Government can fix the amount of imports to be imported into the country during any particular year

3. Applying *import licence* to limit the amount of imports

4. *Borrowing* loans from abroad to finance the BOP deficit

5. *Devaluation* of the local currency to make imports expensive

6. Encouraging *foreign investors* in the country, who in turn bring foreign exchange

7. Encouraging *foreign tourists* to come to the country and bring foreign exchange

8. Giving *incentives* to local producers of exports, e.g. loans, to make them competitive in the world market

9. *Export compensation scheme* – compensating exporters who incur losses when exporting goods to encourage them to remain in business

10. *Foreign exchange control* – giving foreign exchange to some importers of essential goods and denying importers of luxuries

EXCHANGE RATE

This is the price of one currency in terms of other currencies, e.g.

    1 US$ = Kshs. 70/-

There are two types of exchange rates:

1. Flexible/floating exchange rate
2. Fixed exchange rate

Flexible Exchange Rate

This is the exchange rate determined by the market forces of demand and supply of foreign currencies in the money market. This exchange rate keeps on fluctuating.

Fixed Exchange Rate

This is fixed by the Government and in this case there is no appreciation or depreciation.

DEPRECIATION

When there is an increase in exchange rate, e.g. 1 US$ = Kshs. 100/-, it is said that the local currency has depreciated. This means that the value of the local currency has fallen.

Causes of Depreciation

1. When there is a decrease in exports which leads to a low demand for the local currency and the price

decreases

2. Low number of tourists coming into the country
3. Decrease in the number of foreign investors
4. Government intervention in the money market, through the Central Bank, can devalue the local currency

Advantages of Depreciation

1. Discourages imports because they become expensive
2. Encourages exports
3. May lead to improvement in the balance of payment as the level of imports decreases

Disadvantages of Depreciation

1. May lead to imported inflation because imports become expensive
2. May lead to the closing down of local industries which rely on imported raw materials
3. The trading partners may decide to depreciate their currencies
4. The closing down of industries will lead to unemployment

APPRECIATION

When the exchange rate decreases, e.g. 1 US$ = Kshs. 30/, the local currency is said to have appreciated.

Appreciation means the value of the local currency has risen.

Reasons for Appreciation

1. The Government, through the Central Bank, may decide to appreciate the local currency
2. Increased demand for exports, leading to an increase in demand for the local currency. As a result the price of the local currency increases
3. Increase in the number of tourists to the country
4. Increase in the number of foreign investors in the country

Disadvantages of Appreciation

1. Encourages imports as they become cheaper
2. Discourages exports
3. May lead to the closing down of industries because of low exports, which will lead to unemployment
4. It leads to an unfavourable balance of payments as imports increase and exports decrease
5. Discourages foreign tourists
6. Discourages foreign investment

Advantages of Appreciation

1. Encourages local industries that rely on imported raw materials
2. May create employment for the locals

ECONOMIC INTEGRATION

This occurs when a group of countries in a particular region come together and enter into an agreement aimed at promoting free trade. They do so by forming *common markets* or *customs unions* or *trading blocs*, removing trade barriers such as bans, tariffs, quotas, etc. Examples of these are COMESA, ECOWAS, EU, EAC, AU, etc.

Advantages of Economic Integration

1. Consumers get a variety of goods produced in other countries
2. It promotes good relationships among countries
3. Consumers get goods at lower prices because goods are tax free
4. Importation of raw materials becomes easy
5. It leads to increased trade and firms enjoy economies of scale due to large-scale production
6. Competition among countries leads to production of high-quality products
7. It promotes specialization among countries
8. Member countries become a stronger economic unit

when bargaining with other countries

9. It may lead to employment among countries, as factors of production, such as labour, move freely

Disadvantages of Economic Integration

1. Some countries import more than they export, which leads to an unfavourable balance of payments in the affected country

2. Some countries will dump cheap goods in other countries

3. Unfair competition among countries may lead to closing down of industries in the affected countries

4. Some Governments see it as a loss of Government revenue, e.g. in the form of taxes not levied

Limitations of Economic Integration

1. Differences in currencies create payment problems

2. The existence of different languages makes trading difficult

3. Poor infrastructure, especially roads, affects the movement of people and goods from one country to another

4. Most countries produce similar goods and hence there is no need for integration

5. Political instability such as wars

6. Differences in the levels of economic development

means that some countries will gain more than the others

7. Some countries are dishonest and will go against the trade agreements

Solutions/Measures

1. Countries should come up with a common language, e.g. Kiswahili in the EAC
2. Countries should come up with a common currency, e.g. the Euro, to solve the difference in currencies
3. Improve infrastructure to enable people and goods to move faster
4. Improve technology to ensure that countries are on the same level of development
5. Promote political stability among countries
6. Countries should produce a variety of products – diversification
7. Countries should be honest with each other

Forms of Economic Integration

1. *Free Trade Area* – This is a form of regional integration where member countries agree to reduce barriers among themselves but each country retains its own barriers to trade to non-member countries. This removal of trade barriers may only be on specified commodities

2. *Customs Union* – This is a form of regional integration where member countries remove all trade barriers among themselves but have a common external tariff with respect to non-member countries

3. *Common Market* – This is a type of regional integration where, in addition to meeting the requirements of a customs union, there is free mobility of factors of production among member countries. Restrictions on both trade and factor movements are thus abolished

4. *Economic Union* – This is a level of economic integration where there are joint economic institutions among the member countries to coordinate economic policy, as in the case of the European Union. This requires a complete uniformity in commercial and financial policies, where member countries share a common currency or where each country retains its own domestic currency but members allow a free exchange of these currencies at an agreed rate

CHAPTER NINE

BARTER TRADE, MONEY AND BANKING

BARTER TRADE

Before money was invented people used to exchange goods and services for other goods and services. Such a system is called Barter Trade.

Limitations of Barter Trade

1. *Storage Problem* – This is due to the perishability of some goods, e.g. tomatoes

2. *Transport Problem* – Some goods are heavy and bulky

3. *Lack of Divisibility* – Some traded goods are not divisible, e.g. if 1 goat is equal to 1 sack of maize, then ½ sack of maize is equal to ½ a goat; but a goat cannot be divided in two. Doing so will mean killing the goat

4. *Lack of Measure of Value* – It is difficult to determine how many goats are equal to 1 cow and vice versa

5. *Lack of Standard of Deferred Payments* – It is difficult to pay debts incurred now in future

6. *Lack of Double Coincidence of Wants* – It is difficult

223

to merge the buyer and the seller. If a person having a dog wants to exchange for a cow it is not easy to find a person having a cow willing to exchange it for a dog

MONEY

Money is anything which acts and is generally accepted as a medium of exchange for goods and services. Money is what money does.

Functions of Money

1. *Medium of Exchange* – Money acts as a medium of exchange for goods and services
2. *Unit of Account* – The value of goods and services is calculated and the records kept in terms of money
3. *Store of Value* – Perishable gods can be sold and the money kept for future use
4. *Measure of Value* – The price of a product is the value of that product
5. *Moving Immovable Property* – Money can be used to move immovable property from one place to another; e.g. one can sell a house and buy another elsewhere
6. *Standard of Deferred Payments* – Money acts as a standard of deferred payments, because debts incurred now can be paid in future using money

Characteristics of Good Money

1. *Portability* – Good money should be light enough to enable people to move it around
2. *Acceptability* – Good money should be accepted by all as a medium of exchange for goods and services
3. *Divisibility* – Good money should be capable of division into small units to allow people to buy goods even in small units
4. *Durability* – Good money should be long lasting and not easily defaced or spoilt
5. *Stability* – The value of money should be stable for a long time and not fluctuate over time
6. *Homogeneity* – Different money units should have the same value
7. *Malleability* – The material used should not be easy to print or forge
8. *Cognoscibility* – Good money makes it easier to distinguish genuine money from fake money
9. *Scarcity* – Money should be limited in supply and people should work hard to earn money for it to have value

Disadvantages of using money as a medium of exchange

1. Money can easily be stolen
2. Money can be forged

3. Money is scarce, hence not everybody may get it to use as a medium of exchange
4. Money sometimes loses value due to changes in price
5. Money in the form of notes may not be durable

Types of Money

1. *Liquid Cash* – This is the money that can be used as a medium of exchange for goods and services on the spot and this is mainly notes and coins
2. *Near Money Assets* – This is the money that cannot be used as a medium of exchange for goods and services on the spot but can be converted into liquid cash on short notice; e.g. cheques, shares, bank deposits etc.
3. *Money Substitutes* – This is money that cannot be used as a medium of exchange on the spot but can act as a store of value; e.g. credit cards, visa cards, ATMs, etc. This is also known as plastic money

Money Supply

This term refers to the total money stock present in the economy at a particular moment.

It consists of:

M0 = Coins and notes in circulation

M1 = MO + demand bank deposits held by commercial

banks

M2 = money in fixed deposits

M3 = Near money assets, such as cheques

M4 = Money held by non-bank financial institutions e.g. NHIF, Building Societies, Insurance Companies, NSSF, etc

Money supply data are recorded and published, usually by the government or the central bank of the country. Public and private sector analysts have long monitored changes in money supply because of the belief that it affects the price level, inflation, the exchange rate and the business cycle.

There is strong empirical evidence of a direct relationship between money-supply growth and long-term price inflation, at least for rapid increases in the amount of money in the economy.

Some economists argue that the money supply is endogenous, that is it is determined by the workings of the economy, not by the central bank, and that the sources of inflation must be found in the distributional structure of the economy.

Money is used as a medium of exchange, a unit of account, and as a ready store of value. Its different functions are associated with different empirical measures of the money supply. There is no single "correct" measure of the money supply. Instead, there are several measures, classified along a spectrum or continuum between narrow and broad monetary aggregates. Narrow measures include only the most liquid assets, the ones most easily used to spend (currency, checkable deposits). Broader measures add less liquid types of assets (certificates of deposit, etc.).

Factors Determining Money Supply

1. *Government* – In most countries the Government, through the Central Bank, determines money supply
2. *Interest Rates* – When the interest rates are high the supply of money is low and vice versa
3. *Cash Reserve Ratio* – This is the amount commercial banks are supposed to keep, which cannot be lent out. When the ratio is high then money supply is low
4. *Compulsory Deposit Requirement* – Commercial banks are required to deposit some money with a central bank. When the deposits are high the supply of money is low
5. *Public desire to hold money in cash* – If the public desires to hold money in cash, supply is low

Demand for Money

Demand for money is the amount of money the public wishes to hold in the form of notes, coins, and bank deposits. The demand for money is an ante-concept because it tells us the amount of money people wish to have but is not what they actually have. There are various theories that explain the determinants of demand for money.

1. The Keynesian Theory of Demand For Money

2. The Classical Theory of Demand For Money

Keynesian Theory of Demand for Money

According to Keynes, people demand money for three reasons/motives:

1. Transaction Motive
2. Precautionary Motive
3. Speculative Motive

Transaction Motive

People demand money to meet their day-to-day transactions or needs, e.g. to buy food, pay for transport, pay for raw materials etc. At any time people should have enough money to meet such needs. The amount of money held for the transaction motive varies from individual to individual but depends on:

1. ***Price Level*** – The higher the price level the higher the demand for the transaction motive

2. ***Income Level of Individuals*** – The higher the income the higher the expenditure, hence the higher the demand

3. ***Spending Habits of Individuals*** – Some people are very generous and produce a high demand for money. Misers will have a low demand for money for this purpose
4. ***Marginal Propensity to consume*** – If the MPC is high then demand will be high
5. ***Marginal Propensity to sell*** – If this is high then demand will be high

Precautionary Motive

People demand money to meet unexpected events because of uncertainties about the future such as sickness, deaths, visitors etc.

Precautionary demand for money depends on:

1. Income level
2. Family size
3. Age of individual
4. Status (Marital, Societal etc.)

Speculative Motive

Speculative demand for money is based on the desire to earn profit from the market if one knows what the future will bring. People demand money to invest in bonds, shares, etc. Speculative demand for money depends on the interest rates. As the interest rate increases, speculative demand for money also increases.

Demand for Money

Money is necessary to carry out transactions and it provides liquidity. This creates a trade-off between the liquidity advantage of holding money and the interest advantage of holding other assets. The demand for money is a result of this trade-off regarding the form in which a person's wealth should be held.

The demand for money increases with the level of nominal output price level (times real output) and decreases with the nominal interest rate. The real demand for money is defined as the nominal amount of money demanded divided by the price level.

Quantity Theory (Classical Theory)

The most basic "classical" transaction motive can be illustrated with reference to the Quantity Theory of Money. According to the equation of exchange $MV = PY$, where M is the stock of money, V is its velocity (how many times a unit of money turns over during a period of time), P is the price level and Y is real income. Consequently, PY is nominal income or in other words the number of transactions carried out in an economy during a period of time. Rearranging the above identity and giving it a behavioural interpretation as a demand for money.

Say's Law of Markets

The problem in the world of ideas, particularly in the social sciences, is that the insight behind old ideas can get lost as new ideas crowd the intellectual landscape. Such misunderstandings are frequently more than just simple errors; they can have profound effects on our theories of the social world, our interpretations of history, and our proposals for policy. Say's Law of Markets has been fundamentally misunderstood by economic theorists and laypersons alike, and to explore some of the consequences of this misunderstanding.

Say's Law is frequently understood as supply creates its own demand, as if the simple act of supplying some good or service on the market was sufficient to call forth demand for that product. It is certainly true that producers can undertake expenses, such as advertising, to persuade people to purchase a good they have already chosen to supply, but that is not the same thing as saying that an act of supply necessarily creates demand for the good in question. This understanding of the law is obviously nonsensical as numerous business and product failures can attest to. If Say's Law were true in this colloquial sense, then we could all get very rich just by producing whatever we wanted.

Say's Law is supposed to be saying that the aggregate supply of goods and services and the aggregate demand for goods and services will always be equal. He was supposed to have been saying that this equality would occur at a point where all resources are fully employed. Thus, on this view, the Classical economists supposedly believed that markets always reached this full-employment equilibrium. In one sense this is trivially true. If we compare the actual (ex post) quantities of goods bought (demanded) and sold (supplied) they will always be equal. Whatever is sold by one person is bought by another. Presumably, however, Keynes thought the Classical economists meant something else, perhaps more along the lines of market economies will never create general gluts or shortages because the income generated by sales will always be sufficient to purchase the quantity of goods available to buy. There is a strong sense in which this is true, but by itself it does not assure that full employment will take place because obvious examples of significant unemployment and unsold goods can easily be pointed to. And, in fact, this is what critics of Say's Law have done. By pointing to the various recessions and depressions that market economies have experienced, they claim to show that Say's Law was at the very least naive and probably downright wrong.

What Say Said

Say writes: "it is production which opens a demand for products. Thus, the mere circumstance of the creation of one product immediately opens a vent for other products. Say was making the claim that production is the source of demand. One's ability to demand goods and services from others derives from the income produced by one's own acts of production. Wealth is created by production not by consumption. My ability to demand food, clothing, and shelter derives from the productivity of my labour or my non-labour assets. The higher (lower) that productivity, the higher (lower) is my power to demand.

"All power to demand is derived from production and supply. . . . The process of supplying—i.e., the production and appropriate pricing of services or assets for replacement or growth—keeps the flow of demands flowing steadily or expanding." If I sell my services as a computer technician, it is presumed that my resulting demands will be for goods and for services other than those of a computer technician (or something similar). In particular, Say's Law has nothing to do with equilibrium between aggregate supply and aggregate demand, but rather it describes the process by which supplies in general are turned into demands in general. It is always the level of production which determines the ability to demand.

Production Must Come First

This process can be seen in the differences between small, poor, rural towns and wealthier suburban areas. In the small town, the fact that less value is being produced by residents means that their ability to demand goods and services is correspondingly limited.

The selection of products, the number and diversity of sellers, and the degree of specialization among producers is quite limited. In the wealthier suburb, there is an amazing array of products, with a large number of diverse sellers all offering very specialized goods. Perhaps most important is that in the wealthier area, there is a greater degree of competition, as the market can support multiple sellers of particular goods given the level of wealth being generated by producers. Say points out that this explains why a seller will likely get more business as one among a large number of competitors in a big city than the sole seller of an item in the more sparsely populated countryside.

The key to understanding Say's Law of Markets is that it is production that must come first. Demand, or consumption, follows from the production of wealth.

Money is an intermediate good that enables us to buy the things we ultimately desire. However, we have to be careful to remember that what enables us to purchase is not the possession of money, but the possession of productive assets that can fetch a money's worth on the market. When we sell that asset (or our labour services) we receive wealth in the form of money. As we spend that money, we demand from the wealth our production created. However, because we do not spend all of our wealth that we temporarily store as money but choose to continue to hold some of it in the monetary form, the demand for current goods and services will not precisely match the value of what has been produced, as some money remains in the producers' possession. Thus, it looks as though, given the existence and use of money, Say's Law, even rightly understood, leaves open the possibility that aggregate demand is insufficient to purchase what has been supplied.

However, if the monetary wealth is stored in the form of bank-created money, such as a checking accounts (but not Federal Reserve Notes), then that withheld consumption power will be transferred to those who borrow money from the bank that created it. The money I leave sitting in my checking account is the basis for my bank's ability to lend to others. The power to consume that I choose not to utilize by leaving my production-generated wealth as money is transferred to the borrower. When she spends her loan, her addition to aggregate demand fills in for the missing consumption demand resulting from my decision to hold money. There is, therefore, no excess or deficiency in aggregate demand, as long as the banking system is free to perform this process of turning the saving of depositors into the spending of borrowers. Say's Law of Markets cannot be fully appreciated unless one understands the working of the banking system and its role in intertemporal coordination.

All Markets Are Money Markets

Because all market exchanges are of goods or services for money, all markets are money markets, and the only way there can be an excess supply or demand for goods is if there is an opposite excess supply or demand for money. Take the more obvious case of a glut of goods, such as one might find in a recession. Say's Law, properly understood, suggests that the explanation for an excess supply of goods is an excess demand for money. Goods are going unsold because buyers cannot get their hands on the money they need to buy them despite being potentially productive suppliers of labour. Conversely, a general shortage, or excess demand for goods, can only arise if there is an excess supply of the thing goods trade against, which can only be money. Recessions and inflations are, therefore, fundamentally monetary phenomena, as Say's Law points us in the direction of looking at what is going on in the production of money to explain the breakdown of the translation process of production into demand.

Unlike Keynesian critics of Say's Law of Markets who saw deficient aggregate demand resulting from various forms of market failure as causing economic downturns, we have argued that a more accurate understanding of Say's Law suggests that there is no inherent flaw in the market that leads to deficient aggregate demand, nor is the existence of real-world recessions a refutation of the Law. Rather, once we understand the role of money in making possible the translation of our productive powers of supply into the ability to demand from other producers, we can see that the root of macroeconomic disorder is most likely monetary, as too much or too little money will undermine that translation process. Despite having been dismissed in the onslaught of the Keynesian revolution, Say's Law, when properly understood both in its original meaning and its relationship to the banking system, remains a powerful insight into the operations of a market economy.

Liquidity Preference/Liquidity Trap

Keynes and other economists believe that the demand for money depends on the interest rate. As the interest rate increases, fewer people are willing to hold money in the form of cash but prefer to keep it in other forms such as bonds so as to earn profits. On the other hand, when the interest rate falls to a certain level, the demand for money increases, because people will prefer to hold money in cash form instead of investing in other forms, because there is not much profit to be earned. When the interest rate is low people prefer liquid cash and this is referred to as Liquidity Preference or Liquidity Trap.

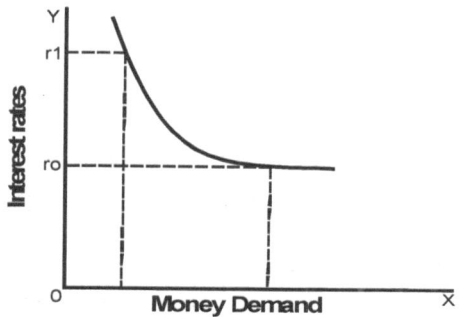

BANKING

A bank is any institution which accepts deposits from those who have excess money, borrows money from the public, lends money to the public, safeguards the money received, makes money available to the owners and performs other banking services.

Types of Banks

1. Central Banks
2. Commercial Banks
3. Specialized Banks
4. Savings Banks
5. Merchant Banks

Central Bank

This is the highest bank in the country, which controls commercial banks and is usually owned by the Government (two well-known exceptions to this convention are the Bank of England and the Federal Reserve Bank in the USA).

Features of the Central Bank

1. Usually owned by the Government
2. Usually managed and controlled by the Government
3. Aim is not to make profit
4. Does not compete with commercial banks
5. Does not deal directly with the public
6. Has a monopoly on issuing currency
7. Banker to the Government

Functions of the Central Bank

1. *Issues Currency* – It is the only bank that has a monopoly on printing notes and minting coins. It ensures that there is the right amount of money in circulation

2. *Advisor to the Government* – It advises the Government on viable projects to invest in and on monetary policies to take to solve problems, e.g. inflation

3. *Banker to the Government* – It receives deposits on behalf of the Government, e.g. in the form of taxes. All ministries pay their workers through the central bank

4. *Lender to the Government* – It gives loans to the Government and raises revenues on its behalf

through the sale of Government securities, e.g. treasury bills

5. *Lender of last resort* – When commercial banks are in financial crisis, they approach the central banks for loans to prevent them from collapsing

6. *Controls commercial banks* – It advises commercial banks on the interest rate to charge on loans. All commercial banks are required by the central bank to keep part of the deposits they receive in the form of cash in a reserve. This is referred to as the Cash Reserve Ratio

7. *Banker to commercial banks* – All commercial banks are required by law to deposit some money with the central bank, where such accounts remain frozen. This is called the Compulsory Deposits Requirement

8. *Control of foreign exchange* – It gives permission to commercial banks and other financial institutions to pay foreign traders. This is to ensure that the right amount of money flows out of the country

9. *Banker to international agencies* – It acts as a banker to international agencies such as the World Bank, the IMF, other central banks etc.

10. *Controls credit* – It ensures that the right amount of money is in circulation to avoid inflation or deflation.

It ensures that commercial banks lend the right amount of money to the public

MONEY/CREDIT CREATION

Money creation (also known as credit creation) is the process by which the money supply of a country or a monetary region is increased.

Most of the money supply is in the form of bank deposits. Bank loans may increase the quantity of broad money to more than the amount of base money issued by the central bank. Governmental authorities, including central banks and other bank regulators, can use policies such as reserve requirements, and capital adequacy ratios to limit the amount of broad money created by commercial banks.

Central banks may also introduce new money into the economy by issuing coins and notes, and by using "expansionary monetary policies" such as the purchase of financial assets (quantitative easing) or loans to financial institutions.

Money issued by central banks is called base money, or reserves, while money issued by commercial banks or other intermediaries is termed broad money.

Central banks monitor the amount of money in the economy by measuring monetary aggregates such as M2. The effect of monetary policy on the money supply is indicated by comparing these measurements on various dates. For example, in the United States, money supply measured as M2 grew from $6.407 trillion in January 2005, to 18.136 trillion in January 2009.

Money Creation by the Central Bank

Monetary policy regulates a country's money supply, the amount of broad currency in circulation. Almost all modern nations have central banks such as the United States Federal Reserve System, the European Central Bank (ECB), and the Central Bank of Kenya for conducting monetary policy. Charged with the smooth functioning of the money supply and financial markets, these institutions are generally independent of the government executive.

The primary tool of monetary policy is open market operations: the central bank buys and sells financial assets such as treasury bills, government bonds, or foreign currencies from private parties. Purchases of these assets result in currency entering market circulation, while sales of these assets remove currency. Usually, open market operations are designed to target a specific short-term interest rate. For example, the U.S. Federal Reserve may target the federal funds rate, the rate at which member banks lend to one another overnight. In other instances, they might instead target a specific exchange rate relative to some foreign currency, the price of gold, or indices such as the consumer price index.

Other monetary policy tools to expand the money supply include decreasing interest rates by fiat; increasing the monetary base; and decreasing reserve requirements. Some other means are: discount window lending (as lender of last resort); moral suasion (cajoling the behaviour of certain market players); and "open mouth operations" (publicly asserting future monetary policy). The conduct and effects of monetary policy and the regulation of the banking system are of central concern to monetary economics

Money Creation by Commercial Banks

In contemporary monetary systems, most money in circulation exists not as cash or coins created by the central bank, but as bank deposits. Commercial bank lending expands the amount of bank deposits. Through fractional reserve banking, the modern banking system expands the money supply of a country beyond the amount initially created by the central bank, creating most of the broad money in the system.

There are two types of money in a fractional-reserve banking system: currency originally issued by the central bank, and bank deposits at commercial banks

1. *Central bank money* (all money created by the central

bank regardless of its form, e.g., banknotes, coins, electronic money)

2. *Commercial bank money* (money created in the banking system through borrowing and lending) – sometimes referred to as *check book money*

When a commercial bank loan is extended, new commercial bank money is created if the loan proceeds are issued in the form of an increase in a customer's demand deposit account (that is, an increase in the bank's demand deposit liability owed to the customer). As a loan is paid back through reductions in the demand deposit liabilities the bank owes to a customer, that commercial bank money disappears from existence. Because loans are continually being issued in a normally functioning economy, the amount of broad money in the economy remains relatively stable. Because of this money creation process by the commercial banks, the money supply of a country is usually a multiple larger than the money issued by the central bank; that multiple was traditionally determined by the reserve requirements and now essentially by other financial ratios (primarily the capital adequacy ratio that limits the overall credit creation of a bank) set by the relevant banking regulators in the jurisdiction

Money Multiplier

The most common mechanism used to measure this

increase in the money supply is typically called the *money multiplier*. It calculates the *maximum* amount of money that an initial deposit can be expanded to with a given reserve ratio – such a factor is called a *multiplier*. It is the maximum amount of money commercial banks can legally create for a given quantity of reserves.

It is calculated as

$$M = \frac{1}{R}$$

where

M = deposit multiple

R = required reserve ratio.

In the re-lending model, this is alternatively calculated as a geometric series under repeated lending of a geometrically decreasing quantity of money: reserves lead loans. In endogenous money models, loans lead reserves, and it is not interpreted as a geometric series. In practice, because banks often have access to lines of credit, and the money market, and can use day time loans from central banks, there is often no requirement for a pre-existing deposit for the bank to create a loan and have it paid to another bank.

If banks accumulate excess reserves, as occurred in such

financial crises as the Great Depression and the Financial crisis of 2007–2008 – in the United States since October 2008, the relationship between base money and broad money breaks down, and central bank money creation may not result in commercial bank money creation, instead remaining as unlent (excess) reserves. However, the central bank may shrink commercial bank money by shrinking central bank money, since reserves are required – thus fractional-reserve money creation is likened to a string, since the central bank can always *pull* money out by restricting central bank money, hence reserves, but cannot always *push* money out by expanding central bank money, since this may result in excess reserves, a situation referred to as "pushing on a string".

Credit Creation: Meaning and Limitations on Credit Creation

Creation of credit is one of the most outstanding functions of a modern bank. A bank has sometimes been called a factory for the manufacture of credit. Let us see what we mean by credit creation, how it is created by the bank and, finally, whether the power of the banks to create credit is unlimited or it is subject to certain limitations.

What is Credit Creation?

It is an open secret that the banks do not keep cent per cent reserve against deposits in order to meet the demands of depositors. The bank is not a cloak room where you can keep your currency notes or coins and claim those very notes or coins back when you desire. It is generally understood that money received by the bank is meant to be advanced to others. A depositor has to be content simply with the bank's promise or undertaking to pay him back whenever he makes a demand.

This bank is able to do with a very small reserve, because all the depositors do not come to withdraw money simultaneously; some withdraw, while others deposit at the same time. The bank is thus enabled to erect a vast superstructure of credit on the basis of a small cash reserve. The bank is able to lend money and charge interest without parting with cash. The bank loan creates a deposit or, as we have seen above, it creates a credit for the borrower.

Similarly, the bank buys securities and pays the seller with its own cheque which again is no cash; it is just a promise to pay cash. The cheque is deposited in some bank and a deposit is created or credit is created for the seller of the securities. This is credit creation.

Thus, term 'credit creation' implies a situation, to use Benham's words, when "a bank may receive interest simply by permitting customers to overdraw their accounts or by purchasing securities and paying for them with its own cheques, thus increasing the total bank deposits."

Limitations on Credit Creation

From the account of credit creation given above, it would seem that the banks 'reap where they have not sown'. They advance loans or buy securities without actually paying cash. But they earn interest on the loans they give, or earn dividends on the securities they purchase, all the same. This is very tempting. They make profits without investing cash. They would, of course, like to make as much profit, like this, as they can.

But they cannot go on expanding credit indefinitely. In their own interest, they have to apply the brake and they do actually apply it, for it is well known that the profits made by the banks are not very high. The overriding limitation arises from the obligation-of the banks to meet the demands of their depositors.

Benham has mentioned three limitations on the powers of the banks to create credit:

(i) The total amount of cash in the country;

(ii) The amount of cash which the public wishes to hold; and

(iii) The minimum percentage of cash to deposits which the banks consider safe.

As for (i), it may be said that credit can be created on the basis of cash. The larger the cash (i.e. legal tender money), the larger the amount 0f credit that can- be created. But the amount of cash that a bank may have is such to the control of the Central Bank.

Here it may suffice to say that the Central bank has the monopoly of issuing the cash. It may increase it or decrease it, and expand or contract accordingly. The power of the central bank to control currency is thus the controlling influence on the extent of credit that it creates.

The second limitation arises from the habit of the people regarding the use of cash. If people are in the habit of using cash and not cheques, as in India, then as soon as credit is granted by the bank to a borrower, he will draw the cheque and gel cash. When the bank's cash reserve is thus reduced, its power to create credit is correspondingly reduced.

On the other hand, if people use cash only for very small and odd transactions, then the cash reserve of the banks is not much drawn upon, and their power of creating credit remains unimpaired. This is the case in advanced countries like the U.S.A., U.K. and other European countries. There the banks keep only 4-5 per cent cash reserve.

The third limitation is the most important. It arises from the traditional reserve ratio of cash to liabilities which the banks must maintain to ensure their own safety and to maintain the degree of liquidity that is considered desirable. It is clear that when a bank creates a credit or grants a loan, it undertakes a liability.

There is an increase in its liabilities, and there is correspondingly a fall in the reserve ratio. The bank will not let the ratio fall below a certain minimum. When that minimum is reached, the power of the bank to create credit comes to an end. To grant any further credit will be risky unless the bank's experience is reassuring enough to permit the adoption of a lower percentage. Then that would become the limit.

To these may be added the fourth limitation: The bank cannot create credit without acquiring assets (in this case the borrower's promise to pay or some security). An asset is a form of wealth. Thus the bank only turns immobile wealth into mobile wealth. Hence, as Crowther observes, "the bank does not create money out of thin air, it transmutes other forms of wealth into money."

To sum up: The essential conditions for the creation of credit are that the banks obtain fresh cash reserves, they should be willing to lend and the businessmen should be willing to borrow, and the borrowers should not withdraw the amount of the loan, but be content to leave it in the form of deposits with the bank. The initiative is in the hands of the borrowers. The deposit is, in fact, created not by the amount borrowed, but by the amount not withdrawn.

Liquidity vs. Profitability

Let us now consider the essentials of sound banking. We have seen that a bank can lend large amounts of money on the strength of a small cash holding. That is why this is called 'creation of credit.' If, tempted by easy profits, it carries this practice too far and does not keep adequate reserves, it may get into trouble. Even a small 'rush' on it may land it in the bankruptcy court. Further, if the bank locks up its funds in long-term investments (like factories, lands and houses which cannot be sold at a pinch), it may have to close its doors one day.

We may then conclude that for achieving soundness

(a) A bank should not advance funds for speculation

(b) It should not invest heavily in industrial undertakings which yield returns only after long periods

(c) It should not lend very large sums of money to an individual borrower or a particular group of borrowers; if they fail, the bank may have to face ruin

(d) It should maintain a high ratio of cash to deposits, loans and advances. Its other reserves should be as liquid as possible.

Thus, on the one side are profits and on the other reserves. High reserves mean less profit. The bank has to follow a path midway between the two extremes. It should strike a happy compromise between liquidity on the one side and profitability on the other.

It must keep sufficient liquid assets so that it may be able to meet the demands of the depositors. If the bank itself speculates, it may have to face disaster one day. The early history of joint-stock banking in India is full of examples where a bank had to close doors on account of its speculative activities.

There is no fixed principle about the proportion of reserves to liabilities. In the last resort, the amount of reserve depends upon the normal demands of a bank's customers. To meet sudden calls— and no one can predict them—the bank's investments should be as liquid as possible so that they can be easily converted into cash.

Nowadays every bank has to keep a percentage of its deposits with the Central Bank of the country. These balances, called bankers' deposits, are as good as money in the bank's own till. The Central Bank uses them as a handle to control its member banks and the total issue of credit in the country. They are also used to help member banks in an emergency, if otherwise they are sound.

It is seen that in countries, where the people are educated and bank- minded, the ratio of reserves to advances is lower than in backward countries. In the U.K., this ratio sometimes falls as low as 3 per cent while in India it is usually much higher. The ratio is lower in the case of old banks with a reputation than in the case of smaller new banks. Deposit insurance schemes are intended to inspire faith among the people in the banking system and thus give it strength and stability.

Methods of Credit Control (Monetary Policy Tools)

Monetary policy is a deliberate action taken by the Government, through the central bank, to control money supply and the cost of money – i.e. the interest rate – to move the economy in the required direction. The following tools are used.

1. *Bank interest rate policy* – When there is excess money in circulation the central bank will instruct commercial banks to increase interest rates on loans. This makes loans from central banks expensive and discourages the public from borrowing

2. *Cash reserve ratio* – When there is excess money supply the central bank increases the cash reserve ratio among commercial banks. This ensures that commercial banks have less money to lend to the public

3. ***Compulsory deposits*** – When there is excess money supply the central bank will increase the compulsory deposit requirements among commercial banks. This will ensure that commercial banks have less money to lend to the public

4. ***Selective credit control*** – When there is excess money supply the central bank would advise commercial banks to approve loans to some projects and deny others

5. ***Open market operations (OMO)*** – This involves the buying and selling of Government securities (e.g. treasury bills) to the public in the open markets. When there is excess money supply the Government, through the central bank, sells the treasury bills. Those who buy them pay cash and thus reduce the amount of money in circulation

6. ***Directives*** – The central bank may order commercial banks to increase interest rates on loans to discourage people from borrowing

7. ***Administrative measures/red tape*** – This is when the central bank instructs commercial banks to increase documents and processes in borrowing and this discourages the public from borrowing

8. ***Moral suasion*** – The central bank may request commercial banks to behave in a certain way for the general benefit of the public

Objectives of Monetary Policy

1. To increase employment in the economy
2. To ensure prices are stable in the economy
3. To promote economic growth and development
4. To ensure equilibrium in the balance of payments

Limitations of monetary policy in developing countries

1. Most banks are owned by foreigners, and borrow money easily from the international market
2. Most people are poor and don't have securities to enable them borrow loans from commercial banks
3. Political interference; e.g. during elections a lot of money is printed to win voters
4. In such economies people keep their money at home and not in banks
5. In developing economies, the financial markets are not well developed
6. Ignorance is rampant as most people don't know the services offered by the banks
7. Open economy
8. Corruption
9. Poor saving habits
10. Low demand for credit

Commercial Banks

These are owned by private individuals, operate like limited companies and offer a variety of banking services.

Features of commercial banks

1. Owned by private individuals
2. The aim is to make profits
3. Controlled and managed by private individuals
4. Deal directly with the public
5. Compete among themselves for customers
6. Don't issue currency; i.e. don't print notes and mint coins

Functions of commercial banks

1. Provide loans to the public for various purposes
2. Receive deposits from those who have excess money and keep them safely
3. Provide good means of payments, e.g. cheques
4. Give advice to traders on viable projects and investments
5. Provide safe places for keeping valuable documents, e.g. title deeds
6. Assist in international trade by making payments to overseas traders
7. Give advice to traders on tax matters

Importance of commercial banks in economic growth

1. They help in developing trade and industry by giving loans
2. They create employment
3. They pay taxes to the Government, which leads to increased Government revenue
4. They give loans to various sectors in the economy, which promotes economic growth
5. They advise business people on viable projects to invest in, which leads to better business decisions
6. They promote good saving services among people for investment purposes by giving interest on deposits

FINANCIAL MARKETS

This is a market for funds. It coordinates activities for lenders and borrowers. The financial market is divided in two parts:

1. *Money Market* – This is a market for short-term loans, e.g. bank overdrafts, short-term loans, etc. The main financial institutions in the money market are the central bank, commercial banks, building societies, etc.

2. *Capital Market* – This is a market for long-term loans, e.g. mortgages, debentures, shares, etc.

Money Markets

1. Market for short-term loans
2. Provides loans for short-term projects
3. Interest charged on loans is volatile and keeps on fluctuating
4. Loans are from commercial or central bank
5. Financial institutions are regulated by the central bank

Capital Market

1. Market for long-term loans
2. Provides loans for long-term projects
3. Interest is relatively stable
4. Loans are from development banks
5. They are regulated by the Capital Market Authority

Non-bank Financial Institutions

They exist in both the money market and the capital market. They specialize in borrowing and lending money for investment purposes, which are different from those of commercial banks, e.g. insurance companies, building societies, NSSF, etc.

Role of Non-Bank Financial Institutions

1. They offer competition to commercial banks, which leads to improved services in the financial market for lenders and borrowers
2. They provide a variety of financial instruments, e.g. mortgages, which has led to the development of financial markets
3. They offer loans to borrowers at lower interest rates
4. They assist where commercial banks have failed, e.g. giving mortgage loans
5. They provide employment to people, thus improving living standards
6. They pay taxes to the Government, which helps the country to achieve economic growth
7. Some engage in development projects like building houses, which they sell to their clients at lower prices

Differences between Commercial Banks and Non-Bank Financial Services

1. Commercial banks operate cheque accounts while non-bank financial firms do not operate cheque accounts with the central bank
2. Commercial banks operate bank accounts with the central bank while non-bank financial institutions do not

3. Some deposits in commercial banks, e.g. current accounts, are non-interest bearing, while all deposits in non-banking institutions are interest bearing
4. Commercial banks can create credit while non-bank financial firms do not have this facility

WORLD FINANCIAL INSTITUTIONS

International Monetary Fund (IMF)

The IMF was established in 1947 to help reconstruct the shattered economies after the Second World War. The main objectives of the IMF are:

1. To ensure there is a stable exchange rate among member countries
2. To reduce disequilibrium balance of payments in international trade by selling foreign exchange to member countries
3. To promote international monetary policies cooperation
4. To promote investment of capital in poor countries by encouraging export of capital from rich countries to poor ones
5. To facilitate the expansion of balanced growth in international trade

Functions of IMF

1. It advises member countries on economic and monetary policies

2. It buys and sells foreign currencies from and to member countries

3. It lends to member countries for development purposes

4. It lends to member countries to help them eliminate disequilibrium balance of payments

5. It provides technical assistance to member countries to prepare and implement various projects

6. It provides international finance to maintain exchange rate stability

Limitations of IMF

1. It has failed to achieve stable exchange rates among member countries

2. It has insufficient capital to meet the requirements of all member countries

3. It is dominated by rich and advanced countries while the poor countries have no say in decision making

4. It discriminates when lending; poor countries don't get loans easily

5. Most policies, such as structural adjustments, have been set by developed countries

World Bank

This bank came to existence during the Bretton Woods Conference held in 1944. The aim of the World Bank is to help reconstruct and develop the economies of member countries.

Objectives of World Bank

1. To provide loans to poor countries and other countries for development purposes
2. To help reconstruct and develop member countries by facilitating investment capital for productive purposes of economies devastated by the 2nd world war
3. To encourage poor countries to develop their productive resources by providing them with investment capital
4. To help improve the standard of living among member countries
5. To promote long-term balanced growth in international trade by maintaining balanced terms of trade

Functions of World Bank

1. Advances loans to member countries to help them lay down foundation of sound economic growth, e.g. in agriculture

2. Provides technical assistance to member countries by sending experts to survey resources, preparing and implementing projects etc.
3. Helps member countries in solving economic problems, e.g. balance of payment (BOP) disequilibrium, by giving them loans
4. Provides loans to member countries for development purposes
5. Encourages industrial development in poor countries by providing loans, technical assistance etc.

Limitations of World Bank

1. It has insufficient financial resources to meet all requirements of member countries
2. The bank discriminates against Asian and African countries when lending
3. The bank is dominated by Western rich countries while poor countries have no say in decision making
4. It charges high interest rates on loans, making loans expensive for poor countries
5. It provides loans to developing countries mainly for agricultural development and not industrial development
6. Poor countries find it difficult to repay the loans in international/foreign currencies, a condition set by the World Bank

CHAPTER TEN

PUBLIC FINANCE

This consists of Government revenue and public (Government) expenditure. This chapter shows how revenue is raised and spent. The word public refers to general people and the word finance means resources. So Public Finance means resources of the masses, how they are collected and utilized. Thus, it is the branch of economics that studies the taxing and spending activities of government. It is that branch of general economics which deals with the financial activities of the state or government at national, state and local levels. Public finance is the study of the role of the government in the economy. It is the branch of economics which assesses the government revenue and government expenditure of the public authorities and the adjustment of one or the other to achieve desirable effects and avoid undesirable ones.

The discipline of public finance describes and analyses government services, subsidies and welfare payments, and the methods by which the expenditures to these ends are covered through taxation, borrowing, foreign aid and the creation of money.

It was Adam Smith who gave a detailed account of the

problems of 'public finance' and recognized the close connection between science of finance and the theory of economics. Following Smith, other classical economists went on writing on one issue or the other in the field of 'public finance'. According to Findlay Shirras "Public finance is the study of principles underlying the spending and raising of funds by public authorities". According to H.L Lutz "Public finance deals with the provision, custody and disbursement of resources needed for conduct of public or government function." According to Hugh Dalton "Public finance is concerned with the income and expenditure of public authorities, and with the adjustment of the one to the other.

Scope

Public finance not only includes the income and expenditure of the government but also the sources of income and the way of expenditure of various government corporations, public companies and quasi government ventures. Thus, the scope of public finance extends to the study of independent bodies acting under the government's direct and indirect control. The Scope of public finance includes:

1. Public Revenue

Public finance deals with all those sources or methods through which a government earns revenue. It studies the principles of taxation, methods of raising revenue, classification of revenue, deficit financing etc.

2. Public Expenditure

Public expenditure studies how the government distributes the resources for the fulfilment of various expenses. It also studies principles that the government should keep in view while allocating resources to various sectors and effects of such expenditure.

3. Public debt

It deals with borrowing by the government from internal and external sources. At any time, government may exceed its revenue. To meet the deficit, government raises loans. The study of public finance focuses on the problems of raising loans and the methods of repayment of loans.

4. Financial/Fiscal administration

The scope of financial administration is wider. It covers all the financial functions of the government. It includes drafting and sanctioning of the budget, auditing of the budget, etc. Financial administration is concerned with the organization and functioning of the government machinery responsible for performing the various financial functions of the state. The budget is the master financial plan of the government.

5. Economic Stabilization and Growth

In the present times, public finance is mainly concerned with the economic stability and other related problems of a country. For the attainment of these objectives, the government formulates its fiscal policy comprising of various fiscal instruments directed towards the economic stability of the nation.

6. Federal Finance

Distribution of the sources of income and expenditure between the central and the state governments in the federal system of government is also studied as the subject matter of the public finance. This branch of public finance is popularly known as Federal Finance.

Functions of Public Finance

The functions of public finance all activities with regard to collection of revenue and expenditure on various activities. Earlier theories public finance narrow definition of the functions to be carried out by public authorities. It is clear that the area of state activity has enlarged over the past two decades which increased the functions and scope of public finance.

1. Economic activities of the state

The scope of public finance was confined to the traditional functions of the state, that is, provision of defence, law and order, justice and civic amenities. But with the emergence of welfare states the scope of public finance was broadened public finance now includes the use of the budget as a tool to correct distortion in the economy, to mobilise resources, to maintain price stability create employment prevent market failure, achieve growth equity and maximize social welfare.

2. Functional Finance

The government should maintain a reasonable level of aggregate demand at all times by using the budget. Most developed economies followed functional finance policies in order to control trade cycles. Developing countries followed such policies to promote economic growth.

3. Fiscal Operations

The scope of public finance includes fiscal operations and their objectives. Fiscal operations refer to raising public revenue, spending to achieve certain goals and financial administration. For such operations, the government uses fiscal tools like taxation, public expenditure and public debt.

The following are the objectives of fiscal operations;

1. Allocation of resources

The most important objectives of fiscal operations is to determine how the Country's resources will be allocated to different sectors of the economy in order to achieve predetermined goals. The national budget determines how funds are allocated to different heads of expenses. The policy of public expenditure is used by the government to directly undertake resource allocation for different sectors. On the other hand, the government can use taxation and subsidies to indirectly influence resource allocation.

2. Distribution

Fiscal operations can be effectively used affect the distribution of national income and resource Taxation and public expenditure policies are used by the government to reduce inequalities. Progressive direct taxation imposes heavier burden on the rich than the poor. Public expenditure on social infrastructure and subsidies on food housing, health and education help reduce income inequality.

3.Stabilisation

Developed economies experience business cycles. Economic stability implies absence of sharp cyclical movements in the form of booms and depressions. To bring about such stability, counter-cyclical fiscal operations are adopted. To counter depression and recession, government expenditure is increased to generate employment and taxes are reduced to encourage consumption and investment. During inflation, public expenditure is reduced and taxes are raised.

4. Economic growth

In developing and underdeveloped economies, the objectives of fiscal operations are more promotional in nature. The basic focus of fiscal operations in such economies is the use of budgetary operations to achieve growth and development. This is done by encouraging capital formation and investments through public expenditure and tax incentives to private sectors

Economic Role of the Government

In the narrowest sense, the government's role in the economy is to help correct market failures, or situations where private markets cannot maximize the value that they could create for society. This includes providing public goods, internalizing externalities, and enforcing competition

There are five economic functions of government

1. Providing the legal structure
2. Maintaining competition
3. Redistributing of income
4. Reallocating of resources
5. Promoting stability

Sources of Government Revenue

1. Taxes – these are the main source of Government revenue
2. Fines imposed on law breakers
3. Fees paid for using Government Services
4. Internal and external loans
5. Donations and grants
6. Selling Government Properties
7. Leasing Government Properties
8. Profit from Government-owned businesses
9. Duties imposed on products such as imports

TAXES

TAXATION

Theories of Taxation

The economists have put forward many *theories or principles of taxation* at different times to guide the state as to how justice or equity in taxation can be achieved. The main theories or principles in brief, are:

Benefit Theory

According to this theory, the state should levy taxes on individuals according to the benefit conferred on them. The more benefits a person derives from the activities of the state, the more he should pay to the government. This

272

principle has been subjected to severe criticism on the following grounds:

Firstly, If the state maintains a certain connection between the benefits conferred and the benefits derived. It will be against the basic principle of the tax. A tax, as we know, is compulsory contribution made to the public authorities to meet the expenses of the government and the provisions of general benefit. There is no direct quid *pro quo* in the case of a tax.

Secondly, most of the expenditure incurred by the slate is for the general benefit of its citizens, It is not possible to estimate the benefit enjoyed by a particular individual every year.

Thirdly, if we apply this principle in practice, then the poor will have to pay the heaviest taxes, because they benefit more from the services of the state. If we get more from the poor by way of taxes, it is against the principle of justice?

The Cost of Service Theory:

Some economists were of the opinion that if the state charges actual cost of the service rendered from the people, it will satisfy the idea of equity or justice in taxation. The cost of service principle can no doubt be applied to some extent in those cases where the services are rendered out of prices and are a bit easy to determine, e.g., postal, railway services, supply of electricity, etc., etc. But most of the expenditure incurred by the state cannot be fixed for each individual because it cannot be exactly determined. For instance, how can we measure the cost of service of the police, armed forces, judiciary, etc., to different individuals? Dalton has also rejected this theory on the ground that there's no quid pro qua in a tax.

Ability to Pay Theory

The most popular and commonly accepted principle of equity or justice in taxation is that citizens of a country should pay taxes to the government in accordance with their ability to pay. It appears very reasonable and just that taxes should be levied on the basis of the taxable capacity of an individual. For instance, if the taxable capacity of a person A is greater than the person B, the former should be asked to pay more taxes than the latter. Ability-to-pay taxation is a progressive taxation principle that maintains that taxes should be levied according to a taxpayer's ability to pay. This progressive taxation approach places an increased tax burden on individuals, partnerships, companies, corporations, trusts, and certain estates with higher incomes.

It seems that if the taxes are levied on this principle as stated above, then justice can be achieved. But our difficulties do not end here. The fact is that when we put this theory in practice, our difficulties actually begin. The trouble arises with the definition of ability to pay. The economists are not unanimous as to what should be the exact measure of a person's ability or faculty to pay. The main viewpoints advanced in this connection are as follows:

(a) *Ownership of Property:* Some economists are of the opinion that ownership of the property is a very good basis of measuring one's ability to pay. This idea is out rightly rejected on the ground that if a person earns a large income but does not spend on buying any property, he will then escape taxation. On the other hand, another person earning income buys property, he will be subjected to taxation. Is this not absurd and unjustifiable that a person, earning large income is exempted from taxes and another person with small income is taxed?

(b) *Tax on the Basis of Expenditure*: It is also asserted by some economists that the ability or faculty to pay tax should be judged by the expenditure which a person incurs. The greater the expenditure, the higher should be the tax and *vice* versa. The viewpoint is unsound and unfair in every respect. A person having a large family to support has to spend more than a person having a small family. If we make expenditure. as the test of one's ability to pay, the former person who is already burdened with many dependents will have to' pay more taxes than the latter who has a small family. So, this is unjustifiable.

(c) *Income as the Basics*: Most of the economists are of the opinion that income should be the basis of measuring a man's ability to pay. It appears very just and fair that if the income of a person is greater than that of another, the former should be asked to pay more towards the support of the government than the latter. That is why in the modern tax system of the countries of the world, income has been accepted as the best test for measuring the ability to pay of a person.

Proportionate Principle

In order to satisfy the idea of justice in taxation, J. S. Mill and some other classical economists have suggested the *principle of proportionate in taxation*. These economists were of the opinion that if taxes are levied in proportion to the incomes of the individuals, it will extract equal sacrifice. The modern economists, however, differ with this view. They assert that when income increases, the marginal utility of income decreases. The equality of sacrifice can only be achieved if the persons with high incomes are taxed at higher rates and those with low income at lower rates. They favor progressive system of taxation, in all modern tax systems.

Rates of Taxation

A marginal tax rate is the tax rate an individual would pay on one additional dollar of income. Thus, the marginal tax rate is the tax percentage on the last dollar earned. ... With a flat tax, by comparison, all income is taxed at the same percentage, regardless of amount.

How do you calculate the tax rate?

The most straightforward way to calculate effective tax rate is to divide the income tax expenses by the earnings (or income earned) before taxes. For example, if a company earned $100,000 and paid $25,000 in taxes, the effective tax rate is equal to $25,000 \div 100,000$ or 0.25

In a tax system, the tax rate is the ratio (usually expressed as a percentage) at which a business or person is taxed. There are several methods used to present a tax rate: statutory, average, marginal, and effective. These rates can also be presented using different definitions applied to a tax base: inclusive and exclusive.

Statutory

A statutory tax rate is the legally imposed rate. An income tax could have multiple statutory rates for different income levels, where a sales tax may have a flat statutory rate. The statutory tax rate is expressed as a percentage and will always be higher than the effective tax rate.

Average Tax Rate

An average tax rate is the ratio of the total amount of taxes paid to the total tax base (taxable income or spending), expressed as a percentage.

In a proportional tax, the tax rate is fixed and the average tax rate equals this tax rate. In case of tax brackets, commonly used for progressive taxes, the average tax rate increases as taxable income increases through tax brackets, asymptote to the top tax rate. For example, consider a system with three tax brackets, 10%, 20%, and 30%, where the 10% rate applies to income from $1 to $10,000, the 20% rate applies to income from $10,001 to $20,000, and the 30% rate applies to all income above $20,000. Under this system, someone earning $25,000 would pay $1,000 for the first $10,000 of income (10%); $2,000 for the second $10,000 of income (20%); and $1,500 for the last $5,000 of income (30%). In total, they would pay $4,500, or an 18% average tax rate.

Marginal Tax Rate

A marginal tax rate is the tax rate an individual would pay on one additional dollar of income. Thus, the marginal tax rate is the tax percentage on the last dollar earned. In the United States in 2016, for example, the highest marginal federal income tax rate was 39.6%, applying to earnings over \$415,050. Earnings under \$415,050 that year had a lower tax rate of 35% or less.

The marginal tax rate on income can be expressed mathematically as follows:

where t is the total tax liability and i is total income, and Δ refers to a numerical change. In accounting practice, the tax numerator in the above equation usually includes taxes at federal, state, provincial, and municipal levels. Marginal tax rates are applied to income in countries with progressive taxation schemes, with incremental increases in income taxed in progressively higher tax brackets.

In economics, one theory is that marginal tax rates will impact the incentive of increased income, meaning that higher marginal tax rates cause individuals to have less incentive to earn more. This is the basis of the Laffer curve theory, which theorizes that population-wide taxable income decreases as a function of the marginal tax rate, making net governmental tax revenues decrease beyond a certain taxation point.

With a flat tax, by comparison, all income is taxed at the same percentage, regardless of amount. An example is a sales tax where all purchases are taxed equally. A poll tax is a flat tax of a set dollar amount per person. The marginal tax in these scenarios would be zero.

Implicit Marginal Tax Rate

For individuals that receive means tested benefits, benefits are decreased as more income is earned. This is sometimes described as an implicit tax.[5] These implicit marginal tax rates can exceed 90%[6] or even greater than 100%.[7] Some economists argue that these issues create a disincentive for work or promotion and may result in a structural income inequality.

Effective Tax Rate

The term *effective tax rate* has different meanings in different contexts. Generally, its calculation attempts to adjust a nominal tax rate to make it more meaningful. It may incorporate econometric, estimated, or assumed adjustments to actual data, or may be based entirely on assumptions or simulations.

The term is used in financial reporting to measure the total tax paid as a percentage of the company's accounting income, instead of as a percentage of the taxable income. International Accounting Standard 12, define it as income tax expense or benefit for accounting purposes divided by accounting profit. In Generally Accepted Accounting Principles (United States), the term is used in official guidance only with respect to determining income tax expense for interim (e.g. quarterly) periods by multiplying accounting income by an "estimated annual effective tax rate", the definition of which rate varies depending on the reporting entity's circumstances.

In U.S. income tax law, the term is used in relation to determining whether a foreign income tax on specific types of income exceeds a certain percentage of U.S. tax that would apply on such income if U.S. tax had been applicable to the income.

The popular press, Congressional Budget Office, and various think tanks have used the term to mean varying measures of tax divided by varying measures of income, with little consistency in definition.

Investors usually modify a statutory marginal tax rate to create the effective tax rate appropriate for their decision.

For example: If capital gains are only taxed when realized by a sale, the effective tax rate is the yearly rate that would have applied to the average yearly gain so that the resulting after-tax profit is the same as when all taxed at statutory rates on sale. It will be lower than the statutory rate because unrealized profits are reinvested without tax.

For example: When dividends are both taxed as income, and also generate a tax credit in the UK and Canadian system, the effective tax rate is the net effect of both - the net tax divided by the actual dividend's value.

For example: When contributions are made to Tax Deferred

Accounts the reduced tax base will result in reduced taxes calculated at the statutory marginal rate. But the reduction in the tax base may also affect qualification for other government benefits. The difference in those benefits is added to the numerator to increase the effective marginal rate due to the contribution.

Characteristics of a Good Tax System

A good tax system should meet five basic conditions: fairness, adequacy, simplicity, transparency, and administrative ease. Fairness, or equity, means that everybody should pay a fair share of taxes. There are two important concepts of equity: horizontal equity and vertical equity.

Characteristics of an Effective Tax System

A good tax system should meet five basic conditions: fairness, adequacy, simplicity, transparency, and administrative ease.

Although opinions about what makes a good tax system will vary, there is general consensus that these five basic conditions should be maximized to the greatest extent possible.

Fairness, or equity, means that everybody should pay a fair share of taxes. There are two important concepts of equity: horizontal equity and vertical equity.

282

Horizontal equity means that taxpayers in similar financial condition should pay similar amounts in taxes.

Vertical equity is just as important, however. Vertical equity means that taxpayers who are better off should pay at least the same proportion of income in taxes as those who are less well off. Vertical equity involves classifying taxes as regressive, proportional, or progressive.

While no system of taxes is perfect, it is important to seek horizontal equity because taxpayers must believe they are treated equally. It is just as important to seek vertical equity so government does not become a burden to low-income residents.

Adequacy means that taxes must provide enough revenue to meet the basic needs of society. A tax system meets the test of adequacy if it provides enough revenue to meet the demand for public services, if revenue growth each year is enough to fund the growth in cost of services, and if there is enough economic activity of the type being taxed so rates can be kept relatively low.

Simplicity means that taxpayers can avoid a maze of taxes, forms and filing requirements. A simpler tax system helps taxpayers better understand the system and reduces the costs of compliance.

Transparency means that taxpayers and leaders can easily

find information about the tax system and how tax money is used. With a transparent tax system, we know who is being taxed, how much they are paying, and what is being done with the money. We also can find out who (in broad terms) pays the tax and who benefits from tax exemptions, deductions, and credits.

Administrative ease means that the tax system is not too complicated or costly for either taxpayers or tax collectors. Rules are well known and fairly simple, forms are not too complicated, it is easy to comply voluntarily, the state can tell if taxes are paid on time and correctly, and the state can conduct audits in a fair and efficient manner. The cost of collecting a tax should be very small in relation to the amount collected.

Types of Taxes

Regressive tax: A tax is regressive if those with low incomes pay a larger share of income in taxes than those with higher incomes. Almost any tax on necessities, such as food purchased at a grocery store, is regressive because lower income people must spend a larger share of their income on these necessities and thus in taxes.

Proportional tax: A tax is proportional if all taxpayers pay the same share of income in taxes. No taxes are truly proportional. Property taxes often come closest since there is typically a close relationship between a household's income and the value of the property in which they live. Corporate income taxes often approach proportional because one rate applies to most corporate income.

Progressive tax: A progressive tax requires higher-income individuals to pay a higher share of their income in taxes. The philosophy behind progressive taxes is that higher income people can afford and should be expected to provide a bigger share of public services than those who are less able to pay.

Direct and Indirect Taxes

In most countries, taxes are collected from taxpayers using two methods. The most common methods of tax collection are direct and indirect methods. The two methods result in two types of taxes: direct and indirect taxes. The taxes are based on incidence and impact on the taxpayer.

Incidence of tax is about who endures the tax burden while impact of tax is about who the tax is imposed on. In some taxes, incidence and impact are borne by the same person while in other taxes, the impact and incidences are borne by different people.

What Is Direct Tax?

In direct tax, incidence and impact are on the same person. The tax is imposed on one person and the person pays the tax. Hence, the tax is demanded from the same person that it is imposed on. Therefore, the tax burden cannot be transferred to another person. For example, in Kenya, there is tax on rental income. The landlord collects the rental income, calculates the tax and pays the rental income tax direct to the government. Hence, the person the tax is imposed on has the responsibility to pay the tax. The person pays the tax direct to the government. However, there are cases where agents are appointed by the government. For example, employers are agents of the government for collection of tax on employment income (PAYE). The employers remit the PAYE directly to the government on behalf of the employees.

Examples of Direct Taxes

In every country, there are different types of direct taxes imposed on the taxpayers by the governments. The taxes are imposed on various income generation activities such as employment and business. The taxpayer pays the taxes depending on the activities that they engage in. The following are some examples of direct taxes that a government may impose on various activities in the country:

1. Corporate income tax – where a person earns an income from operating a business.

2. Personal income tax – where an individual person

earns an income other than from employment income and does not have a corporate business.

3. Employment income – where a person earns income from employment activities.

4. Capital gains tax – where a person gains an income on transfer of a property.

5. Rental income tax – where a person earns an income from renting commercial or residential properties, land or securities.

6. Property tax – tax paid by a person who owns a property in a certain locality.

7. Gift taxes – a tax paid by a person for receiving a gift.

Advantages of direct taxes to the taxpayers

1. Positive impact on equitable distribution of wealth

Under direct taxes, the wealthy taxpayers are expected to pay more tax. Hence, taxpayers especially the low-income earners are happy to know that the wealthy taxpayers pay more taxes. The taxpayers see equitable distribution of the country's resources.

2. Tax certainty

To the taxpayer, direct taxes have advantage of certainty. The certainty is in terms of the time to pay the tax, the manner of tax payment and the amount of taxes to pay. This certainty enables the taxpayer to plan adequately. For example, in Kenya every employee is aware that PAYE is payable for all employment income earned every month.

3. Simple application

Application of some types of direct taxes is simple and easy. Most of direct taxes are levied on simple flat tax rates. In addition, there are some taxes that are not remitted on a monthly basis but periodically.

3. Creates public awareness

Direct taxes create public awareness among the persons who pay the tax to the government. This awareness is created because the taxpayer pays the tax directly to the government and not through third parties. Therefore, the taxpayer becomes more interested in the activities of the government especially on how the tax revenue is utilized.

Disadvantages of direct taxes to the taxpayer

1. Direct pain

Taxpayers pay the taxes directly to the government from their incomes, salaries, allowances etc. Though the taxes are desirable, most taxpayers are pained when paying direct taxes. The taxpayers deduct a certain percentage of their earnings and remit it to the government as direct tax.

2. Complex procedures

Sometimes, in complying with the requirements of direct taxes, there are complex formalities in the procedures relating to the source of the income. This is because taxpayers have various sources of income. Most taxpayers engage in various income generating activities to make ends meet.

3. Arbitrary tax rates and interpretation

The tax authorities set the tax rates for direct taxes. The tax authorities have freedom to determine the tax rates without any reference to anyone. In addition, the tax authorities set the tax laws that guide the implementation of the same direct taxes in the country.

4.Requires money to pay

When direct taxes are due to be paid, they must be paid. Otherwise, the taxpayers will pay fines, penalties and interests. Direct taxes are paid after the person has earned the income not in the process of earning the income. Sometimes, the taxpayers use the income earned for other more pressing needs especially when it is business income.

5.Cannot be avoided

It is almost impossible to avoid direct taxes because the activities that the governments impose the taxes on are a necessity. For example, employment and business activities are necessary activities for survival. Thus, the people cannot avoid the taxes.

6.Inconvenient

Direct taxes are inconvenient to the taxpayer. The taxpayer

must ensure that they track all their sales. In addition, the taxpayers must ensure that they have captured all business expenses. The expenses must have a direct relation with the income generated. Further, the taxpayers must collect the money to pay the taxes when due. This is inconveniencing to the taxpayer hence disadvantageous.

Indirect Taxes

There are several examples of indirect taxes. The following are some of the taxes:

1. Value-added tax
2. Excise tax
3. Sales tax

Advantages of indirect taxes to taxpayers

The following are some of the advantages of indirect taxes to taxpayer.

1.Convenient

In some countries, payment of indirect taxes is very convenient. This is because indirect taxes are paid only when a good or a service is consumed. In addition, unless a person is a registered tax agent, they do not put aside time to go and pay the indirect taxes. They pay the tax as they continue doing their normal day to day activities such as consumption of goods and services (e.g lunch), purchase of various items for the business etc.

2.Less burden-some

Indirect taxes are not paid in lump sum but in small quantities as consumption and purchase of goods or services takes place. For example, if one is consuming goods or services that are subject to indirect taxes such as VAT, they will pay according to their consumption each time throughout the month. Therefore, indirect taxes are less burden-some. This cannot be compared with direct taxes such as income tax on employment income where the tax is deducted once at the end of the months and remitted to the tax authority.

3.Manageable

Indirect taxes are not paid as a one-off payment but are continuously paid as the taxpayers consumes or purchases the goods and services. For example, VAT is paid along the supply chain. The final VAT burden is borne by the final consumer who pays the 100 % VAT. This is only for what they consume as final consumers.

4.Less Painful

Most prices of the goods or services that are subject to indirect taxes are tax inclusive. For example, most goods and services are VAT inclusive. Hence, taxpayers may not be aware about the indirect taxes that they are paying. Therefore, the buyers of the goods and services do not experience the pain of paying the indirect taxes. Hence, they may not feel the pain of paying the taxes.

5.Ability

Consumers of goods and services that are subjected to indirect taxes pay the tax according to their ability to consume or purchase the goods and services. The consumers can limit their consumption according to their ability to pay.

6.What are the disadvantages of indirect taxes to taxpayers?

Disadvantages of Indirect Taxes

1.Negative effect on taxpayers

Indirect taxes results in increased prices. When indirect taxes such as VAT and excise taxes are imposed on such items as alcoholic drinks, food items, manufacturing raw materials, electricity, bottled water etc. the prices increase. However, the price increment is borne by the final consumer. Hence, indirect taxes result in increase in prices and affects taxpayers negatively.

2.Regressive tax

Majority of the indirect taxes have a flat tax rate. This makes indirect taxes regressive in nature because the tax systems do not distinguish between persons in the different social strata. The tax rates are the same irrespective of whether the consumer is wealthy or poor.

3.Effects on employment

When indirect taxes are imposed, they increase the prices of goods and services. When the prices of goods and services increase, the demand will decrease. This will affect production negatively. When the producers are faced with reduced markets for their goods and services, they can no longer afford to employing their workers. The only alternative that the employers have is to lay off the workers. This affects employment negatively.

4.Higher cost of living

When indirect taxes are imposed, the prices of goods and services will increase in the whole country. This negatively affects the production cost of goods and services since the workers will demand for higher salaries and wages which will result in higher prices of goods and services. The movements in prices result in inflationary pressures in the economy resulting in higher cost of living. This is disadvantageous to the taxpayers.

5.Lack of public awareness

When people pay indirect taxes, they are not aware that they are paying the taxes. For example, when one takes lunch in a restaurant, they pay the bills without even noticing the amount of VAT that they pay. There is no direct effect on the consumers. Hence, their awareness of the taxes is limited. Therefore, indirect taxes do not create public awareness about paying taxes in majority of the taxpayers. This is a disadvantage to the taxpayer.

6.Responsibility to collect tax

Registered taxpayers have the responsibility to collect the indirect taxes along the supply chain. However, the final consumer is the one who bears the tax 100 %. In case the registered taxpayers fail to collect the tax, they are penalized for it. Hence, indirect taxes add extra responsibility to the registered taxpayers.

7.Requirement to maintain records

The government requires that all the registered taxpayers maintain tax records for the tax that they collect on behalf of the government including records for indirect taxes. The taxpayers should maintain the records and submit them to the government when required to do so without any delay.

8.No exemptions

Indirect taxes unlike direct taxes do not have exemptions for low income groups. This often results in injustices on the low-income groups. For example, in Kenya, VAT is at 16 %. Irrespective of the income that one earns, the tax rate remains the same.

Tax Incidence

A tax incidence is an economic term for the division of a tax burden between buyers and sellers. Tax incidence is related to the price elasticity of supply and demand. If demand is more elastic than supply, producers will bear the cost of the tax. In economics, tax incidence or tax burden is the analysis of the effect of a particular tax on the distribution of economic welfare. Tax incidence is said to "fall" upon the group that ultimately bears the burden of, or ultimately has to pay, the tax.

The Role Of Taxation In Developing Economies

1. Resource Mobilisation

Taxation enables the government to mobilise a substantial amount of revenue. The tax revenue is generated by imposing: Direct Taxes such as personal income tax, corporate tax, etc., Indirect Taxes such as customs duty, excise duty, etc.

2. Reduction in Inequalities of Income

Taxation follows the principle of equity. The direct taxes are progressive in nature. Also, certain indirect taxes, such as taxes on luxury goods are also progressive in nature. This means the rich class has to bear the higher incidence of taxes, whereas, the lower income group is either exempted from tax (direct taxes) or has to pay lower rate of duty (indirect taxes) on goods consumed by the masses. Thus, taxation helps to reduce inequalities of income and wealth.

3. Social Welfare

Taxation generates social welfare. The social welfare is generated due to certain undesirable products like alcoholic products, tobacco products and such other products are heavily taxed, which restricts their consumption, which in turn facilitates social welfare. A part of the tax revenue is utilised for social development activities, such as health, education and family welfare, which also improve social welfare as well as social order in the society.

4. Foreign exchange

Taxation encourages exports and restricts imports. Generally, developing countries and even the developed countries do not impose taxes on export items. For instance, in India, exports are exempted from excise duty, VAT, customs duty and other duties.

However, there is customs duty on imported goods. Therefore, taxation helps to: Earn foreign exchange through the promotion of exports.

5. Regional Development

Taxation plays an important role in regional development; Tax incentives such as tax holiday for setting up industries in backward regions, which induces business firms to set up industries in such regions, Tax revenue collected by government is also utilised for development of infrastructure in backward regions.

6. Control of Inflation

Taxation can be used as a tool of controlling inflation. Through taxation, the Government can control inflation as follows: -

1. If inflation is due to high rise in prices of essential items, then the Government may reduce the rate of indirect taxes.

2. If inflation is due to increase in demand, the Government may try to cut down the effective demand by increasing the tax rate. Increase in tax rate may restrict consumption, which may reduce demand, and subsequently inflation may be controlled.

These are compulsory contributions imposed by the Government on people from which no direct benefits are obtained.

Characteristics of a Good Tax System

These are also known as the canons of taxation or principle of taxation

1. *Equality/Equity* – A good tax system should be based on the ability to pay such that the rich pay more than the poor

2. *Economy* – The cost of collecting the taxes should be relatively cheap to enable the Government to obtain maximum revenues

3. *Simplicity* – It should be simple for people to understand why the taxes are collected and how they are spent

4. *Certainty* – The Government should be certain how much revenue it will get to meet its expenditure. Tax payers should be certain as to how much, when, how and what to pay

5. *Convenience* – It must be convenient for the tax payer in terms of what, when, how much and how to pay

6. *Productivity* – It must enable the Government to get maximum revenues for the intended purpose without causing negative effects on the economy, e.g. discouraging people from working hard

7. *Flexibility* – It must be flexible such that it can be increased or decreased when the need arises

8. There should be *no room for tax evasion*

Principle of a Good Tax System

- Equity and fairness
- Certainty
- Convenience of payment
- Economy of calculation
- Simplicity

- Neutrality
- Economic growth and efficiency
- Transparency and visibility

Purpose/Importance of Taxation

1. To help Government to raise revenue
2. To promote equal distribution of wealth by taxing the rich more and using the money to help the poor
3. To protect local infant industries through import duties
4. To limit the consumption of harmful goods such as beer, cigarettes etc.

GOVERNMENT EXPENDITURE

This consists of income spent by the Government to provide goods and services to the public. Public expenditure is spending made by the government of a country on collective needs and wants such as pension, provision, infrastructure, etc. Until the 19th century, public expenditure was limited as laissez faire philosophies believed that money left in private hands could bring better returns. Government spending or expenditure includes all government consumption, investment, and transfer payments, Government acquisition of goods and services intended to create future benefits, such as infrastructure investment or research spending, is classed as government investment (government gross capital formation). So, government spending or government expenditure is often divided into three main types: Current Expenditures, Capital Expenditure or Gross Expenditure.

Theories on Government Expenditure

Wagner's Law

Wagner's Law is named after the German political economist Adolph Wagner (1835-1917), who developed a "law of increasing state activity" after empirical analysis on Western Europe at the end of the 19th century. He argued that government growth is a function of increased industrialization and economic development. Wagner stated that during the industrialization process, as the real income per capita of a nation increases, the share of public expenditures in total expenditures increases. The law cited that "The advent of modern industrial society will result in increasing political pressure for social progress and increased allowance for social consideration by industry."

Wagner (1893) designed three focal bases for the increased in state expenditure. Firstly, during industrialization process, public sector activity will replace private sector activity. State functions like administrative and protective functions will increase. Secondly, governments needed to provide cultural and welfare services like education, public health, old age pension or retirement insurance, food subsidy, natural disaster aid, environmental protection programs and other welfare functions. Thirdly, increased industrialization will bring out technological change and large firms that tend to monopolize. Governments will have to offset these effects by providing social and merit goods through budgetary means.

In his Finanzwissenschaft (1883) and Grundlegung der politischen Wissenschaft (1893), Adolf Wagner pointed out that public spending is an endogenous factor, which is determined by the growth of national income. Hence, it is national income that causes public expenditure. The Wagner's Law tends to be a long-run phenomenon: the longer the time-series, the better the economic interpretations and statistical inferences. It was noted that these trends were to be realized after fifty to hundred years of modern industrial society.

Peacock and Wiseman Theory of Public Expenditure

In 1961, Peacock and Wiseman elicited salient shaft of light about the nature of increase in public expenditure based on their study of public expenditure in England. Peacock and Wiseman (1967) suggested that the growth in public expenditure does not occur in the same way that Wagner theorized. Peacock and Wiseman choose the political propositions instead of the organic state where it is deemed that government like to spend money, people do not like increasing taxation and the population voting for ever-increasing social services.

There may be divergence of ideas about desirable public spending and limits of taxation but these can be narrowed by large-scale disturbances, such as major wars. According to Peacock and Wiseman, these disturbances will cause displacement effect, shifting public revenue and public expenditure to new levels. Government will fall short of revenue and there will be an upward revision of taxation. Initially, citizens will engender displeasure but later on, will accept the verdict in times of crisis. There will be a new level of "tax tolerance". Individuals will now accept new taxation levels, previously thought to be intolerable. Furthermore, the public expect the state to heal up the economy and adjust to the new social ideas, or otherwise, there will be the inspection effect.

Peacock and Wiseman viewed the period of displacement as reducing barriers that protect local autonomy and increasing the concentration power over public expenditure to the Central government. During the process of public expenditure centralization, the role of state activities tends to grow larger and larger. This can be referred to the concentration process of increasing public sector activities. Nowadays, the growth in public expenditure has become a compulsion and thus, the disturbance situations matter little.

The Classical V/S the Keynesian Approach of Public Expenditure

The classical economists believe that the government intervention brings more harm than good to an economy and that the private sector should carry out most of the activities. In his Welfare of Nations, Adam Smith (1776) advocated much on the "laissez-faire" economy where the profit motive was to be the main cause of economic developments. According to the classical dichotomy, an increase in the total amount of money leads to a proportionate increase in all money prices, with no change in the allocation of resources or the level of real GDP, which is known as money neutrality. The classical economists assumed that the economy was perfect: it is always at full employment level, wage rate and rate of interest is self-adjusting and as a matter of fact, the budget should always balance as savings is always equal to investment. Since they believe that the economy was always at its full employment level, their objective was certainly not growth.

Following the 1929-30 Great Depression, the classical economists that opposed government interventions, argued that strong trade unions prevented wage flexibility which resulted in high unemployment. The Keynesians, on the other hand, favoured government intervention to correct market failures. In 1936, John Maynard Keynes' (1883-

1946) "General Theory of Employment, Interest and Money", criticized the classical economists to put too much emphasis on the long run. According to Keynes, "we are all dead in the long run". Keynes believed depression needed government intervention as a short-term cure. Increasing saving will not help but spending. Government will increase public spending giving individuals, purchasing power and producers will produce more, creating more employment. This is the multiplier effect that shows causality from public expenditure to national income.

Keynes categorized public expenditure as an exogenous variable that can generate economic growth instead of an endogenous phenomenon. Hereby, Keynes believed the role of the government to be crucial as it can avoid depression by increasing aggregate demand and thus, switching on the economy again by the multiplier effect. It is a tool that bring stability in the short run but this need to be done cautiously as too much of public expenditure lead to inflationary situations while too little of it leads to unemployment.

Maximum Social Advantage

The politics of public expenditure have gained new dimensions, namely welfare maximization. The principle of maximum social advantage is derived from the principle of equi-marginal utility. The law states that a rationale individual will distribute his given money income on two or more goods in such a way, that the marginal utility of the last money spent on either good, is the same. This law is based on ceteris paribus conditions.

Dalton's Condition

According to Dalton, "public expenditure in every direction must be carried just so far that the advantage to the community of a further small increase in any direction is just balance by the disadvantage of a corresponding small increase in taxation and in receipts from any other source of public income. This gives the ideal of both public expenditure and public income". Hereby, there will be a cycle where money collected from the public, directly or indirectly, will go back to them in the form of public expenditure programmes. During this process, taxpayers suffer those benefitting from these social welfare programmes gain. For the population to benefit from these continuous transfers of funds, sacrifice must be less than benefit

Pigou's Condition

In his Economics of Welfare, Professor A. C. Pigou (1932) divided welfare economics into two parts, namely, the production and the distribution. The pigou tax rate is used to internalize negative externalities and taxes are used as subsidy for positive externalities. According to Professor Pigou (1928), the condition of maximum social advantage is that situation in which, "Expenditure should be pushed in a direction to the point at which satisfaction obtained from the last shilling spent is equal to the satisfaction lost in respect of the last shilling paid as taxes to the government." The theory is based upon two assumptions: rational consumers and the principle of equality between marginal social sacrifice and marginal social benefit. Pigou's condition should lead the Net Social Benefit which is the difference between marginal social sacrifice (MSS) and marginal social benefit (MSB).

Musgrave's Condition

Dr. R. A. Musgrave has explained the maximum social advantage differently on diagrams. He believed that the situation of maximum social advantage can be achieved where net social benefit equals zero. In other words, the net social benefit is at maximum when MSB minus MSC equals zero.

Bowen's Model of Public Expenditure

An interesting point by Howard R. Bowen (1943) is that social goods are not equally available to all voters. According to him, since social goods are consumed by all individuals in a community, each of them needs to contribute for the social goods. But as Bowen rightly says, we must in the case of public goods add different individuals' curves vertically. This is so because the capacity to enjoy the social goods is different for different individuals. Since each of them has different valuation of the social goods, we expect them to contribute different amounts. Hereby, the government will produce an amount of social goods equal to the marginal cost of supplying that good, to be equal to the marginal utilities received by the community.

Solow Growth Model

In his classic 1956 article, Robert Solow proposed the study of economic growth basing itself from a standard neoclassical production function. Neoclassical growth theory focuses mainly on capital accumulation and saving-related topics. Assuming there is no technological progress, this would imply that the economy has reached the steady-state equilibrium, where per capita income and capital are constant.

Solow found that the critical elements of GDP growth are technical progress, increased labor supply and capital accumulation. More profound research showed other factors as well to increase GDP growth: availability of natural resources and human capital. As a matter of fact, the income share of human capital is large in industrialized countries. Moreover, the result of high investment ratio (large physical capital stock) might as well increase the GDP growth. On the other hand, Solow residual is the change in total factor productivity which is technical progress. In other words, it means the amount by which output would increase as a result of improvements in methods of production, with all inputs unchanged.

Causes of Growth of Public Expenditure

There are several factors that have led to enormous increase in public expenditure through the years

1) Defence expenditure due to modernization of defence equipment by navy, army and air force to prepare the country for war or for prevention

2) Population growth – It increases with the increase in population, more of investment is required to be done by government on law and order, education, infrastructure, etc. investment in different fields depending on the different age group is required.

3) Welfare activities – welfare, mid-day meals, pension provisions etc.

- Provision of public and utility services – provision of basic public goods given by government (their maintenance and installation) such as transportation.

- Accelerating economic growth – in order to raise the standard of living of the people.

- Price rise – higher price level compels government to spend increased amount on purchase of goods and services.

- Increase in public revenue – with rise in public revenue government is bound to increase the public expenditure.
- International obligation – maintenance of socio economic obligation, cultural exchange etc. (these are indirect expenses of government)

4) Wars and social crises – fighting amongst people and communities, and prolonged drought or unemployment, earthquake, hurricanes or tornadoes may lead to increase in public expenditure of a country. This is because it will involve governments to re-plan and allocate resources to finance the reconstruction.

5) Creation of super national organizations – E.g., the United Nations, NATO, European community and other multinational organizations that are responsible for the provision of public goods and services on an international basis, have to be financed out of funds subscribed by member states, thereby adding to their public expenditure.

6) Foreign aid – Acceptance by the richer industrialised countries of their responsibility to help the poor developing countries has channelled some of the increased public expenditure of the donor country into foreign aid programmes.

7) Inflation – This is the general rise in price level of goods and services. It increases the cost of all activities of the public sector and thus a major factor in growth in money

terms of public expenditure.

8) Total population

9) Price level

10) Level of urbanization

11) Number of projects

12) Natural disasters and calamities such as droughts, disease, etc.

Purpose of Government Expenditure

1. *Protection* – to maintain law and order as well as to protect citizens from external aggression

2. Direct investments, e.g. in industries

3. To provide public goods such as roads, electricity, etc.

4. Social functions, e.g. medical, free education, etc.

5. To promote economic stability, e.g. reduce unemployment

BUDGET

The Government, like any other individual, must prepare an annual budget showing sources of revenues and expenditure. A National Budget is an official budget of a nation that is typically drafted by a Treasury and voted on by a legislative body. National budgets are examined carefully to determine how they will affect the country's budget surplus or deficit. A government budget is an annual financial statement presenting the government's proposed revenues and spending for a financial year that is often passed by parliament. Government budget, forecast by a government of its expenditures and revenues for a specific period of time.

Functions of a National Budget

Allocating resources in conformity with both policies and fiscal targets. This is the main objective of the core processes of budget preparation. In the context of business management, the **purpose of budgeting** includes the following three aspects: A forecast of income and expenditure (and thereby profitability) A tool for decision making. A means to monitor business performance.

The Budget performs five key functions in a County.

1. Allocation function

The Budget guides the development process in the County through resource allocation.

2. Distribution function

The Budget ensures balanced distribution of the County's resources and that wealth is realised through identification of sectors that need renewed focus and affirmative action.

3. Stabilization function

The Budget helps to attain and maintain a desired level of

economic performance in the County. There are some desired levels of stability that citizens require.

4. Fiscal transparency

The Budget ensures transparency, especially in the manner in which public expenditure is managed. Public information provides a clear reflection of the Government's expenditure priorities. It, therefore, forms a basis through which citizens can challenge the County Executive over its stated policies and public announcements.

5. Control function

Budgets are useful because they provide a basis for evaluating performance. Performance evaluation is carried out by comparing actual performance with planned or budgeted performance. The causes of significant deviations from planned performance can then be identified.

Budget Making in Kenya

A government budget is a document presenting the government's proposed revenues, spending and priorities for a financial year. The budget is passed by the legislature, approved by the chief executive and presented by the national or country treasury to the national or county assemblies. It is also a set of procedures by which the government rations resources and controls spending among the various government agencies. The government budget is used as an instrument for economic policy, management and accountability. It is an allocation mechanism that aims to maximise the contribution of public expenditure to national welfare.

Legal Framework and Process

The Constitution of Kenya provides the broad principles of public finance whereas the Public Finance Management Act, 2012 sets out the rules of how the national and county governments can raise and spend money.

County Level Budget Making Process

Section 125 of the Public Finance Management Act, 2012 provides the procedure to be followed in the budget making process at the county level as outlined below:

a) Development of an integrated development planning process, which includes both long term and medium-term planning;

b) Planning for and establishing financial and economic priorities for the county over the medium term;

c) Making an overall estimation of the county government's revenues and expenditure;

d) Adoption of the County Fiscal Strategy Paper;

e) Preparing budget estimates for the county government and submitting estimates to the county assembly;

f) Debate and approval of the budget estimates by the county assembly;

g) Enactment of the appropriation law and any other laws required to implement the county government's budget;

h) Implementation of the county government's budget;

i) Accounting for and evaluating the county government's budgeted revenues and expenditure.

The county treasury has the mandate to prepare and submit to the county executive committee the County Strategy Fiscal Paper for approval. The county executive then submits the County Strategy Fiscal Paper to the county assembly for approval by 28th February each year.

The County Strategy Fiscal Paper contains the strategic priorities and policy goals for the county government, the estimates, expenditure, revenue and borrowing for the next financial year.

The county assembly should then within 14 days consider and adopt the Strategy Fiscal Paper with or without amendments. The county treasury shall consider any recommendations made by the county assembly and publish the Fiscal Paper within 7 days.

The county executive shall also prepare annual cash flow projections for the next financial year by 15th June, to be sent to the Controller of Budget, Intergovernmental Budget and Economic Council and the National Treasury. The county executive member in charge of the county treasury shall submit the budget estimates and other documents together with the draft Bills (for implementation of the county government budget), except the Finance Bill, to the county executive committee for approval by 30th April every year.

Following approval by the county executive committee, the budget estimates shall be submitted to the county assembly for approval. The clerk to the county assembly shall then prepare the budget estimates for the assembly and forward them to assembly and the county executive committee member in charge of the county treasury for comments.

After submission of budget estimates to the county assembly for approval, the county executive committee member in charge of the county treasury shall publish and publicise them. Upon approval, the county executive committee for finance shall prepare and submit the County Appropriation Bill with the approved budget estimates to the county assembly.

It should be noted that the month of May is the period when the county budget committee holds public hearings on the budget. The county assembly shall consider and approve the Appropriation Bill, with or without amendments, and within

90 days after its passing, the assembly shall pass the Finance Bill. On October 30th, the county government must publish the first quarterly implementation report. Section 35 of the Public Finance Management Act and is similar to the process at the county level.

Types of Government Budgets

According to the government, the budget is of three types. It assumed that taxes are the main sources of revenue.

1. Balanced Budget - This occurs when Government expenditure is more than revenue. G>T
2. Surplus Budget This occurs when Government revenue is more than expenditure. T>G
3. Deficit Budget - This occurs when revenue is equal to expenditure. T = G

Most countries experience budget deficit.

1. Balance budget

A government budget is said to be balanced when it is estimated revenues and anticipated expenditure are equal. i.e. government receipts and government expenditure. Well, it implies that the government raises funds in the means of taxes and other means a balanced budget was considered an effective check on extravagant expenditure of the government. The government must exercise financial discipline and should keep its expenditure within the available income. The concept of a balanced budget has been evocated by classical economists like Adam smith. A balanced budget was considered by them as neutral in its effects on the working of the economy and hence they are regarded it as the best. However, modern economists believe that the policy of balance budget may not always be suitable for the economy, for instance during the period of depression, when economic activities are at low level, resulting in unemployment. The government may come to the rescue of the people It can borrow money and spend it on public works. This will increase employment and total demand for goods and services and encourage investment.

2. Surplus budget

When estimated government receipts are more than the estimated government expenditure it is termed as surplus budget. When the government spends less than the receipts the budget becomes surplus that is.

Estimated government receipts > anticipated government expenditure.

A surplus budget is used either to reduce government public debt or increase its savings. A surplus budget may prove useful during the period of inflation. In periods of inflation, although there is greater employment there is also a tendency for prices to rise rapidly. This has to be checked particularly in the interest of those who have more or less fixed income. This inflationary gap can be corrected by lowering the level of effective demand in the economy. It can be corrected by increasing taxes. This would increase the revenue of the government but reduce the purchasing power of the people. As a result, the aggregate demand will fall. This inflation gap can be corrected by lowering the level of public expenditure.

The surplus budget should not be used in a situation other than the inflationary gap as it may lead to unemployment and low levels of output as an economy.

3. Deficit budget

When estimate government receipts are less than the government expenditure. In modern economies, most of the budget are of this nature. that the estimate government receipts < anticipated government expenditure.

A deficit budget increases the liability of the government or decreases its reserves.

A deficit budget may prove useful during the period of depression as economics activities are at a low level. It results in unemployment, business loss and even bankruptcy and inflation etc. The government can borrow money and increase the expenditure on public works through deficit financing. This will increase employment and total effective demand for the goods and also the services which would then encourage investment. Thus, a deficit budget is useful for removing depression and unemployment.

Any country in the world is aiming to avoid deficit budget although the surplus budget is difficult for a country to achieve and that is the reason countries strive for a balanced budget in order to avoid inflation, unemployment, loss or any another consequence.

Medium-Term Expenditure Framework

Medium-Term Expenditure Framework (MTEF) The MTEF is annual, rolling three year-expenditure planning. It sets out the medium-term expenditure priorities and hard budget constraints against which sector plans can be developed and refined. MTEF also contains outcome criteria for the purpose of performance monitoring.

Burden of Public Debt and Its Measurement!

Burden of Internal Debt

It is said that an internal debt has no direct money burden since the interest payment on debt and the imposition of taxation to pay interest to the lenders is simply a transfer of purchasing power from one to another. This means that in case of internal debt, money is borrowed from individuals and institutions within the country.

Repayment (raised from taxation) constitutes just a transfer of resources from one group of persons to another. In other words, these are transfer payments and do not affect the total resources of the community Truly speaking, government collects money through taxation imposed on the richer people who are also the buyers of government bonds.

That is to say, government collects money from the left pocket and pays it back to the right pocket. Thus, under internal debt, since all payments cancel out each other in the community as a whole, there is no direct money burden.

Above all, money collected from internal source of borrowing is usually spent for various developmental activities. Such expenditure results in transfer of resources in the community and, as a result, aggregate resources of the country increase. Thus, there can be no direct money burden of internal debt.

But there is no denying the fact that internal debt involves direct real burden to the community according to the nature of the series of transfer of incomes from taxpayers to the creditors. If we assume that the taxpayers and bondholders are the same persons then there can be no direct real burden of debt. But we know that the taxpayers and the bondholders belong to different income groups in the community. Usually, the bondholders are richer people compared to the taxpayers.

320

Certainly, it is necessary to raise taxation to pay interest on the debt and, the greater the debt, greater the amount of taxation required to provide the interest on it. Ordinarily, taxpayers are poor people. When the government pays interest with principal to the bondholders, it results in the transfer of purchasing power from the poor people to the richer people.

Thus, the payment of internal debt involves redistribution of aggregate income. This results in inequalities in the distribution of income and wealth. This is the direct real burden of debt on the community.

Again, it is argued that taxpayers are generally active people while bondholders are idle, old and inactive ones who live on accumulated wealth. In case of repayment of internal debt, wealth thus gets transferred from the active persons, i.e., taxpayers, to the inactive persons, i.e., bondholders. This certainly adds to the real burden of debt.

Some economists argue that public debt is invariably a burden on the future generation. They argue that when the government borrows, the present generation escapes the burden. After the loan is repaid at a later date with interest, the future generation has to suffer by being forced to pay additional taxes. In other words, the future generation will suffer when the present generation reduces its savings as disposable income declines following a rise in taxation.

However, there are some people who do not agree with this view. They argue that there is no shifting of the basic burden to the future. According to modern economists, the real burden of governmental activities must be borne during the period in which expenditures are made, since, during this period, only resources are diverted from private to public sector use.

Borrowing method affects the future generations in two ways only. To the extent to which public debt reduces capital formation, the stock of capital goods and the potential level of national income in future generations will be less.

Further, the borrowing methods create some problems for the future generations in the form of adverse effects on the economy from the taxes necessary to pay interest and principal, inflationary or deflationary effects of the existence of the debt, etc. Thus, there is no shifting of the basic burden to the future.

According to J. M. Buchanan, during the period in which the governmental activities and borrowing take place, no burden is created, because burden, by nature, implies a compulsory sacrifice. Individuals in most cases voluntarily exchange their liquid funds for government bonds. Thus, the present generation does not feel any burden on them. However, it is a burden on the future generations who pay taxes (compulsorily) for the retirement of public debt. So, we can conclude that the question of shifting the burden of public debt to the posterity or future generation is still an unresolved phenomenon.

Burden of External Debt:

During a given period, the direct money burden of external debt is the interest payment as well as the principal repayment (i.e., debt servicing) to external creditors. The direct real burden of such external borrowing is measured by the sacrifice of goods and services which these payments involve to the members of the debtor country.

There is also indirect money burden of external debt. Loan repayment by the debtor country implies more exports of goods and services to the creditor country. Thus, a debtor country experiences a fall in welfare of the community.

Indirect real burden of external borrowing is crucial. Usually, government imposes taxes to finance external debt. But taxes have disincentive effects. It discourages work-effort and saving. Lower the saving, lower is the capital formation. Thus, external borrowing eats away economic growth since growth largely depends on capital formation. This indirect real burden of external debt is quite similar to internal debt.

Knowing fully well the dangers of borrowing, governments of LDCs are compelled to public borrowing—both from internal and external sources.

Measurement of the Burden of Debt

Usually, burden of debt refers to financial burden of the government. But as it does not indicate true burden, we consider following ratios to estimate the burden of debt:

1. Income-Debt Ratio:

It is estimated as:

size of public debt/national income = D/Y

If Y remains at a very high level, the burden of debt, D, will be insignificant. However, if the ratio becomes high, debt then poses a great burden.

2. Debt-Service Ratio:

This ratio is measured as:

Annual interest payments of borrowing/National income = i/Y

Increase in Y means lower debt-service ratio. However, taxes are collected for the repayment of public debt. Thus, this ratio indicates the necessity of imposing higher taxes.

3. Debt Service-Tax Revenue Ratio:

It is worked out as:

Annual interest payments/Aggregate tax revenue = i/T

An increase of this ratio indicates the financial weaknesses of the government.

Debt Management

This is any strategy that helps a debtor to repay or otherwise handle their debt better. Debt management may involve working with creditors to restructure debt or helping the debtor manage payments more effectively. A debtor may appeal to a debt management company if he/she does not know how to manage the debt himself/herself or if there is so much debt that outside management becomes necessary. It can also be described as a regulation of the size and handling of the structure of the public debt. Actions taken to manage the debt have significant effects on the financial markets because government securities compete with private securities for limited funds in the capital market.

Causes of Budget Deficit

1. In developing countries most people are poor and cannot afford to pay taxes, leading to low tax revenues

2. Natural disasters, leading to increased Government expenditure
3. Poor Government investment strategies (White Elephants)
4. Unnecessary Government spending
5. Political instability, e.g. wars
6. Debt repayment
7. High expectations of receiving loans and grants, which do not materialise
8. Increase in population, which leads to Government spending on public and social goods

FISCAL POLICY

This involves the use of taxes, Government expenditure, public borrowing and public debt management to move the economy in the required direction.

Objectives of Fiscal Policy

1. To achieve full employment in the economy by increasing expenditure on projects
2. To promote equal distribution of income in the economy by taxing the rich more and using the taxes to help the poor
3. To achieve equilibrium in the BOP by restricting imports and promoting exports
4. To ensure price stability in the economy

5. To promote economic growth and development in the economy

GOVERNMENT INTERVENTION

The Government sometimes intervenes in economic operations so as to protect the public, e.g. in the product market, labour market etc.

Objectives of Government Intervention

1. To protect consumers against being exploited by greedy traders who may overcharge
2. To protect producers against being exploited by middlemen who may offer low prices
3. To promote social welfare, e.g. by providing free medical services and free education
4. To ensure that consumers get quality and standard goods through such agents as KBS
5. To protect workers from being exploited by employers by fixing the minimum wage
6. To ensure consumers do not get harmful goods
7. To ensure people get goods all the time by discouraging traders from hoarding

Tools of Government Intervention

1. Price Control – fixing minimum and maximum prices
2. Fixing minimum wages in the labour market

3. Imposing duties to protect local and infant industries

4. Setting rules and regulations to be followed

5. Expenditure, e.g. on public goods

6. Taxes to promote equal distribution of income

7. Public ownership to prevent private monopolies

INFLATION

This means a persistent increase in the general price level of goods and services in the economy over a long period. The cost of living increases and money value falls. It may also mean too much money chasing too few goods. Inflation is basically a rise in prices. A more exact definition of inflation is a situation of a sustained increase in the general price level in an economy. Inflation means an increase in the cost of living as the price of goods and services rise. Inflation leads to a decline in the value of money. Inflation means that your money won't buy as much today as you could yesterday.

Rates of Inflation

1. Creeping inflation – prices rise slowly

2. Walking inflation/Moderate inflation

3. Running inflation

4. Hyper-inflation

Types/Causes of Inflation

Demand Pull

This occurs when there is excess demand for goods and services in the economy over supply and hence the price increases.

Causes

1. Excess money supply chasing few goods
2. Poor weather conditions causing low supply compared to demand
3. Increase in population leading to excess demand, hence increased prices
4. Decreased personal savings
5. Increased incomes from wages and exports
6. Decreased personal taxes

Cost Push

This is caused by increased cost of production of goods and services. Producers who aim at making maximum profits increase product prices to meet the cost.

Causes

1. Increase of taxes on inputs
2. Increased wages as demanded by trade unions

Imported Inflation

Inflation in one country can be transferred to another country through international trade, e.g. an oil price increase in Saudi Arabia may be transferred to Kenya.

Sectoral Inflation

Inflation in one sector, e.g. the agricultural sector, can be transferred to another sector, such as the industrial sector.

Disadvantages of Inflation

1. Discourages savings; people prefer to use their money now rather than save it and use it for the future when prices have increased
2. Lenders of money receive money with less value than when loans were made
3. May lead to political instability, as witnessed by strikes, demonstrations, etc.
4. Government workers cannot get a pay rise during periods of inflation
5. Fixed income earners (e.g. rent receivers) get the same amount of money during inflation
6. May lead to low demand for product; industries will close down, leading to unemployment
7. Hyperinflation may lead to the collapse of the monetary system of trade; barter trade will be preferred

8. Unequal distribution of income and wealth

Advantages/Benefits of Inflation

1. Workers with a strong trade union may receive a pay rise during periods of inflation and after inflation the wages cannot be adjusted downwards
2. Investors may use excess profits to invest in other projects
3. Increased investment will lead to increased employment
4. Economic growth is stimulated through investments
5. Borrowers of money pay money with less value than when they borrowed
6. Traders buy raw materials at low prices, sell goods at high prices and this enables them to make huge profits

Monetary Policies/Measures to Curb Inflation

These are methods that can be used by the central bank to control inflation. Such methods include:

1. Bank interest rate policy
2. Open market operation (OMO)
3. Directives
4. Compulsory deposits requirements
5. Cash reserve ratio

6. Moral suasion
7. Selective credit control
8. Red tape

Fiscal Measures to Curb Inflation

1. Increase personal income taxes, which will reduce disposable income
2. Reduce taxes on inputs so as to make outputs cheap
3. Wage controls, such as maximum wages
4. Price controls
5. Increased production to ensure that there is no shortage

Ways in Which Inflation Inhibits the Ability of Money to Perform Its Functions

1. *As a store of value* – People may prefer to store their wealth in other assets, such as property
2. *As a unit of account* – Because of price variations money cannot be used as a unit of account
3. *As a means of exchange* – People may resort to barter trade or alternatives such as gold
4. *As a standard of deferred payments* – Borrowers gain, but the lenders lose, as the real value of the debt declines

TEST QUESTIONS

1. Describe the conditions necessary for a successful price discrimination practice

2. Explain the main factors that influence the choice of a site for a production firm

3. Describe the major tools of Government intervention in an economy

4. State and explain the key functions of a central bank in an economy

5. Explain the relevance of the concept of national income to an economy

6. Explain various ways in which a country can stimulate private investment in the economy

7. Explain the qualities of good money material

8. Using a schedule and a graph explain the law of diminishing marginal utility and state the assumptions

9. Define indifference curve and state the properties of indifference curves

10. State and explain the applications of indifference curve analysis

11. Define isoquants and explain the assumptions

12. Analyse the properties of isoquants

13. Using a schedule and a graph assess the production possibility

14. Explain why some countries will impose restrictions on trade
15. Outline the concept of consumer sovereignty and discuss its limitations
16. Distinguish between demand-deficient unemployment and frictional unemployment
17. Suggest policy measures that can be adopted to combat unemployment
18. Identify the salient features of a monopolistic competitive market
19. In the context of an oligopoly market, explain the concept of the kinked demand curve
20. Suggest possible economic policies that can be adopted to reduce the balance of payments problems in developing countries
21. Explain the circumstances under which price control is considered
22. Distinguish between balance of payments and balance of trade
23. Differentiate between income consumption curve and price consumption curve
24. Distinguish between the term "leakages" and "injections" as used in the circular flow of national income
25. Discuss the factors that lead to inequalities in the distribution of income and wealth in an economy

26. Identify and explain the causes of budget deficits in developing countries

27. Differentiate between cost push and demand pull inflation

28. "International trade is not beneficial to any country". Discuss

29. Explain the Keynesian unemployment model

30. State and explain the major forms of non-tariff barriers

31. Explain the relevance of National Income Statistics

32. Outline the objectives and functions of the International Monetary Fund (IMF)

33. Explain ways in which a country can attract foreign investors

34. Discuss the Keynesian theory of demand for money

35. Explain the merits of using price mechanism in resource allocation

36. Explain the differences between commercial banks and non-bank financial institutions

37. State the reasons why consumer protection is necessary

38. Explain the main determinants of money supply

39. Explain the principles of a good tax system

40. Define the term "liquidity preference" and discuss the Keynesian view on liquidity preference

41. Explain the factors which cause a shift in the demand

curve

42. Explain the factors which cause a shift in the supply curve
43. Distinguish between individual demand curve and market demand curve
44. Distinguish between monopoly and monopolistic competition
45. Evaluate the Philips curve with the help of a graph
46. Discuss the quantity theory of money (Classical Theory)
47. Assess the Says Law of Market
48. Explain the factors that limit the application of monetary tools in developing economies
49. Highlight the reasons why national debt management is a salient policy issue in developing countries
50. Outline the role of non-bank financial institutions in economic development of a country
51. Outline the applications of indifference curves
52. Describe the conditions necessary for a successful price discrimination practice
53. Define Public Finance and explain its functions
54. Explain 3 Types of Budgets
55. Assess 6 objectives of public expenditure
56. Outline 6 effects of national debt
57. Distinguish between direct and indirect taxes
58. Define public expenditure

59. Evaluate national debt management in Africa
60. Asses the functions of public finance in developing countries
61. Compare and contrast public goods from private goods
62. Explain the functions of the national budget in Kenya
63. Examine the Canons of taxation
64. Assess the composition of public expenditure in Kenya
65. Explain the Medium-Term Expenditure Framework (MTEF)
66. Using a well labelled diagram explain the efficiency Output of a Public Good

REFERENCES

1. Philip Hardwick et al, 1999, *An Introduction to Modern Economics,* Longman Pub Group, London, UK

2. D.N. Dwivedi, 2nd Edition, *Principles of Economics,* S. Chand Publishing, New Delhi, India

3. Dewett K.K., Revised Edition, *Modern Economic Theory,* S. Chand Publishing, New Delhi, India

4. Ddumba J. and Ssentamu 2007, *Basic Economics for East Africa* Fountain Publishers Ltd, Kampala, Uganda

5. Todaro and Smith, *Economic Development,*1994, 12th Edition Pearson, London, England

6. Lipsey R., 1991, *Economics,* Orion Publishing Group, London, UK

7. Ahuja H. L., 2007, *Advanced Economic Theory,* S. Chand Publishing, New Delhi, India

8. Jhingan M.L., 7th Edition, *Micro Economic Theory,* Vrinda Publications (P) Ltd, New Delhi, India

9. Todaro M.P., 1992, *Economics for Developing Countries,* Longman Publishing Group, UK

10. Lipsey R.G., 5th Edition, *An Introduction to Positive Economics,* Orion Publishing Group, London, UK

11. Mudinda R. 2009, *Modern Economics*, Focus Publishers, Nairobi, Kenya

12. King J.E., 1990, *Labour Economics*, Macmillan Education, UK

13. Smith S.W., 2003, *Labour Economics*, Routledge Publishers, UK

MICRO AND MACRO ECONOMICS

UNDERSTANDING THE BASICS OF ECONOMICS

–DR. SAMWEL NYAGUCHA ORESI –

DECEMBER 2014